IMAGINE PICASSO

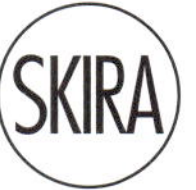
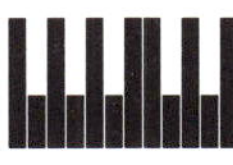
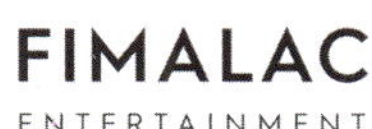

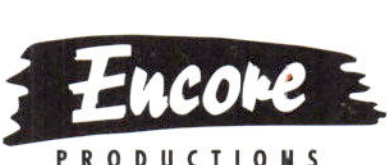

The immersive exhibition "Imagine Picasso" offers a new look at the work of Pablo Picasso. Previewed in the building of La Sucrière in Lyon in 2019, and then in 2021 in Quebec and Vancouver, it continues its journey around the globe.

The creation of this project was meant to answer the essential question: why project this work in Image Totale©?

The aim was to select 200 emblematic paintings from the thousands made by Pablo Picasso and create an ideal exhibition, bringing together in one place the images of *Les demoiselles d'Avignon* (New York), *Guernica* (Madrid), *Portrait de Dora Maar* (Paris), etc.

This adventure was a revolution in the world of immersion, with the implementation of a new protocol. I wanted to create a collective project by surrounding myself with the best. First, Julien Baron, whose years of training at Cathédrale d'Images and then abroad have given him a strong experience in artistic and technical creation. Then, Rudy Ricciotti, the architect who decided to incline the surfaces in order to reinvent verticality and to create a rich experience. Then, the art historian Androula Michael to help understand this colossal artistic production and to provide access to knowledge for all, starting in the educational space at the entrance of the exhibition.

"Imagine Picasso" is the result of a unique dialogue between Pablo Picasso, one of the greatest artists of the 20th century, Rudy Ricciotti, the National Grand Prix of Architecture and the Image Totale© technique.

Thanks to this process of multi-projection, each visitor will wander in the middle of an enchantment of images, where there is neither center nor periphery. The sensitive intelligence of each viewer will allow them to imagine their own Pablo Picasso...

ANNABELLE MAUGER,
Co-Director with Julien Baron of "Imagine Picasso"

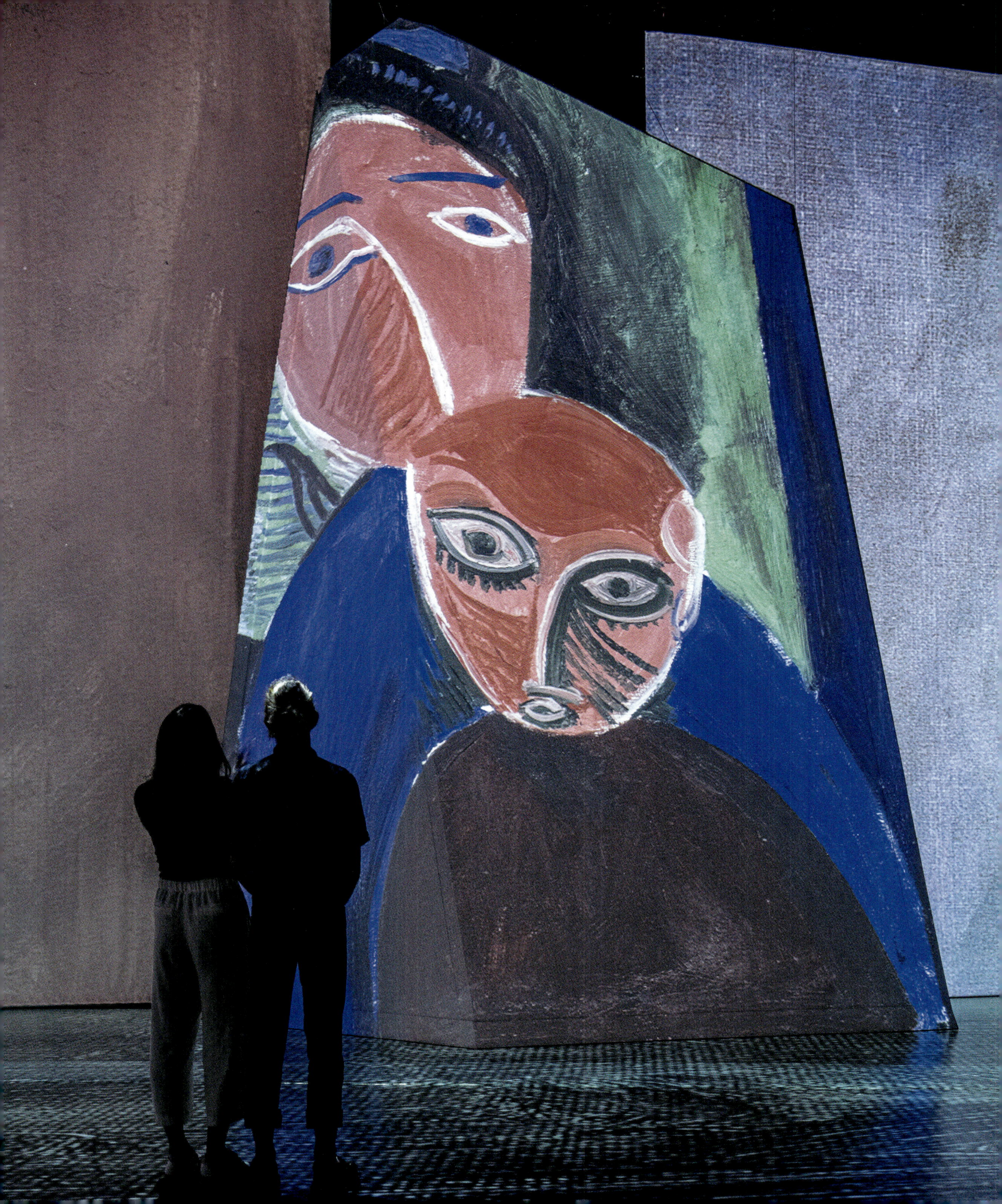

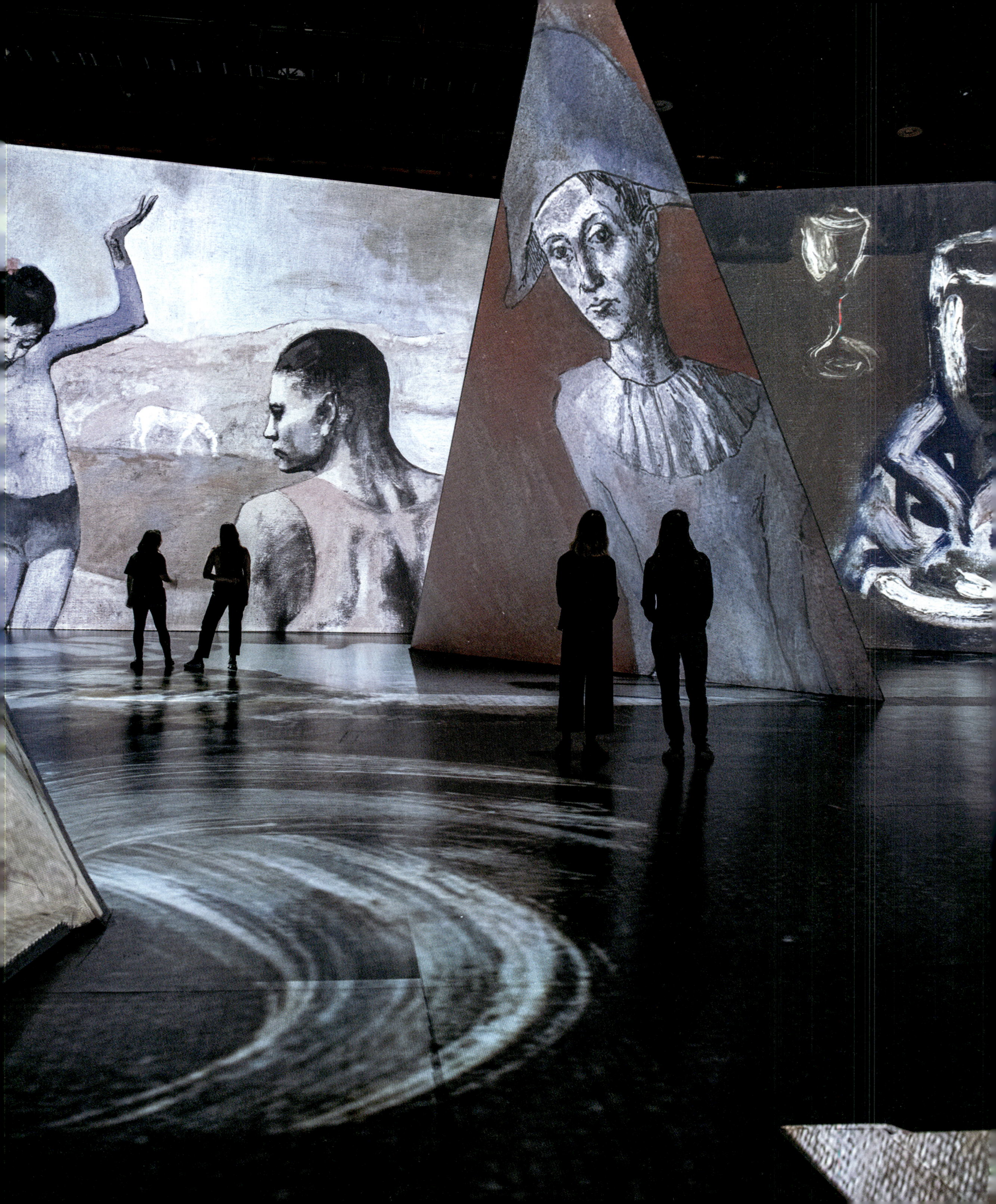

IMAGE TOTALE

Annabelle Mauger and Julien Baron are using the Image Totale© technique pioneered by Albert Plécy for Cathédrale d'Images in 1975. Plécy unleashed the image from its original frame, book, poster or screen to make the most of the vast dimensions of the exhibition space. He did this with the help of architect Hans-Walter Müller, inventor of topoprojection, a forerunner of current projection mapping techniques made possible thanks to new technology. As early as 1977, topo-projection was covering the vast surfaces of the projection site at Carrières des Baux de Provence.

This is the spirit in which Annabelle Mauger and Julien Baron, who worked with these technique at Cathédrale d'Images for several years, are using the narrative process of projection and pushing it further each time.

The Image Totale© principle at the "Imagine Picasso" project can be appreciated in its totality because it creates continuity from a set of images that are linked together and invents a specific type of narrative. The image is projected onto a complex structure, occupying the entire space, to create an immersive experience. The viewers find themselves in the middle of a wonderland of images as if in a daydream. Free from all constraints and routine, they are in a space with no center or periphery; they can then move and look wherever they like as they wander around. The visitors are guided by their own sensitivities, an experience reinforced by the music that also surrounds them.

The immersive exhibition transports the visitors to another world. In Annabelle and Julien's "Imagine" exhibitions the design is reimagined every time depending on the space. From historic venues like La Grande Halle de la Villette in Paris to modern venues such as Singapore's ArtScience Museum, "Imagine" exhibitions open new possibilities in the perception of reality and what can be achieved.

The Image Totale© technique is now being applied to Picasso. Annabelle Mauger has worked with architect Rudy Ricciotti to create a specific setting for this new type of projection that completely changes our perception of the image. Projected in this way, it takes shape on a set which sculpts it, hangs it and leaves it free in terms of movement and direction. The image shows the detail and frees it from traditional constraints. It was a challenge for Annabelle Mauger to find an alternative to the vertical elevation of the images. Rudy Ricciotti's diagonal structures allow unusual projection, neither vertical nor horizontal, but tracing multiple vanishing lines. The overall effect gives a new way of looking at the works of Picasso.

"Imagine Picasso" is not a traditional exhibition of projections; it's a total experience that stands out from other immersive exhibitions at the current time. It is a complex installation of the interaction between a great artist, a great architect and a liberated image.

Picasso himself would have been intrigued by this new type of vision and way of showing his works. As his biographer Pierre Cabanne said, Picasso authorized the audiovisual projection of his paintings in 1971 in Les Halles Baltard: "A remarkable show in which the works of Picasso were shown one after the other on 10 screens in a semi-circle to a captivated audience. Children were delighted and showed their joy at this wild and bizarre kaleidoscope… Because this is perhaps how we should show Picasso: eternally youthful with his incredible and continuous creativity. This people's Picasso, shown in a fractured space entirely occupied and transcended by his genius, is the real Picasso. The technique used at Les Halles allows us to see at a glance the antagonistic and complementary aspects of the same object; it is quite simply the process of cubism in motion (…) Picasso's broken-up style took on epic dimensions on the screens of Les Halles. (Pierre Cabanne, *Le siècle de Picasso*).

The new means of projection made his work more popular. "Imagine Picasso" is a continuation of this.

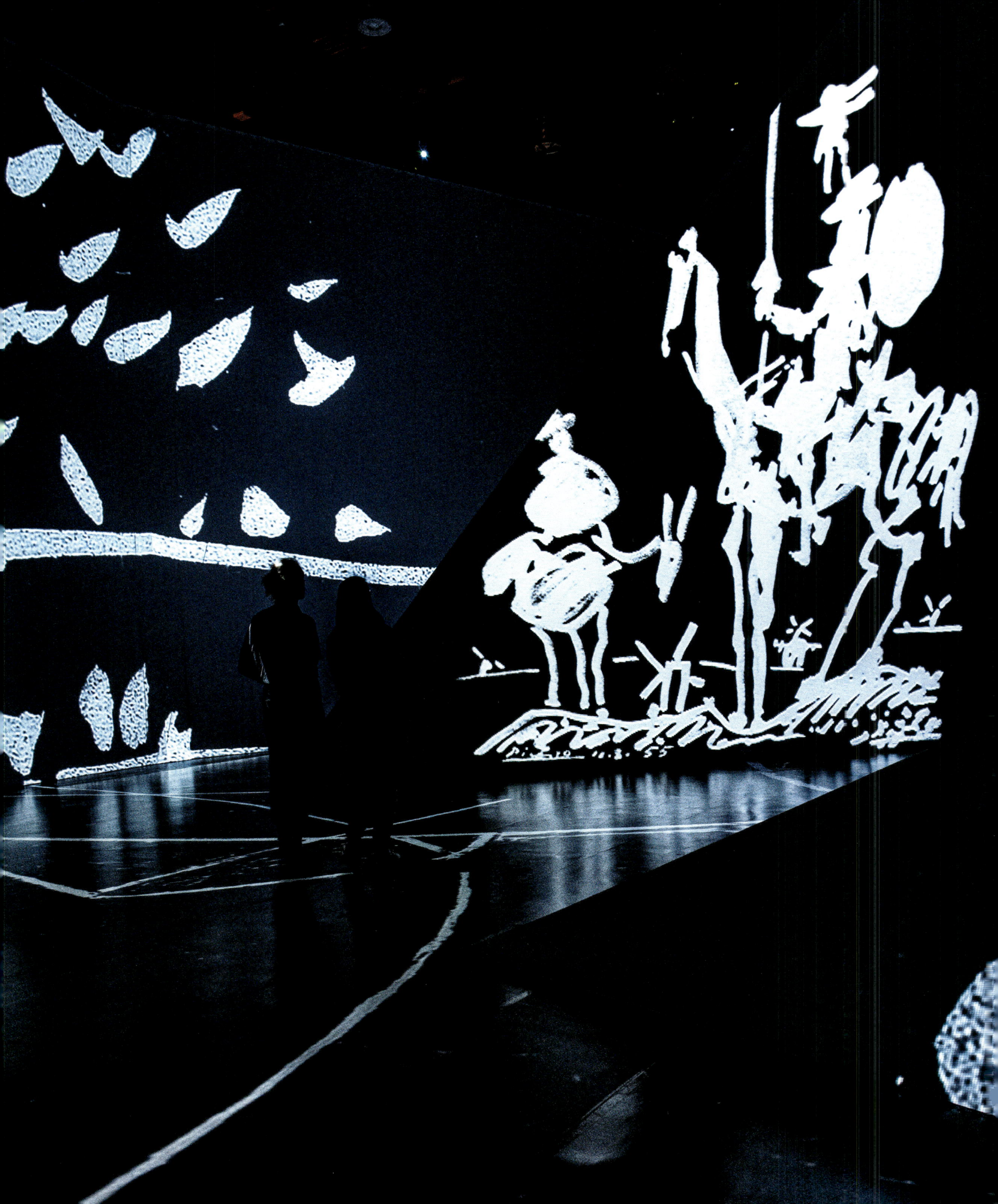

The staging of the "Imagine Picasso" exhibition sprang from the story of a decade-long friendship with Annabelle Mauger and Cathédrale d'Images. I'm an architect, not a scenographer. If I had been guided by logic I would have declined this proposal, but a whiff of adventure on an avant-garde path made me throw caution to the wind.

The "Imagine Picasso" exhibition is not just another commercial regurgitation of a selected accumulation of Picasso's works. We've been there before: the repeated exhibitions of the master's work have become a commercial product, stamped with the seal of commissioners and insurers... little more than a money-making scheme.

This essential exhibition, conceived by Annabelle Mauger and Julien Baron, does not show a single original Picasso piece. What it does do is demystify the relationship between the work and its price, showing Picasso's works as a chain of successive experiments rather than just a few links. This is the greatest virtue of an exhibition which showcases the work of a man who has carried out more than 60,000 "experiments": it shows the sequences, the joints, the jumps, the circular movements of thought. In other words, it shows the journey rather than the destination.

In Carrière des Baux-de-Provence in the 1970s Albert Plécy, a pioneer of removing pictures from their frames, invented the notion of "image totale" and set up the Cathédrale d'Images. He fiddled with his first projectors, found new angles and cleared the caves for the first experiments with gigantic, enveloping and "sculpted" images on the blocks of rock in the belly of the Alpilles mountains. The images were projected at heights of 15 to 17 metres on a single block.

The Cathédrale d'Images was constructed from limestone and clay. Then came the sting, the eviction. The Cathédrale was exiled, Annabelle became a migrant with art in tow. I myself have gypsy origins: we met and it was a good match.

The "Imagine Picasso" exhibition took to the road. Some places were particularly limited in height and the notion of vertical scale (inherent in Les Baux and the roots of Cathedrale d'Images) became obsolete. La Sucrière, the first exhibition venue, had a low ceiling: how could such giant artworks survive in spaces lower than 3.25 meters?

The projection of the image for "Imagine Picasso" would no longer be vertical, the oblique appeared — here I give a nod to my late friend Claude Parent. The sloping projection and inclined supports are a key characteristic of the staging system chosen to maintain the scale of the images. It gives the show a new topography — the image is no longer projected onto the walls, nor on orthogonal planes in a horizontal/vertical direction: the image, still magnified, becomes fleeting in its perception and dynamic in its delivery. "Imagine Picasso" is a wide-awake wandering in a landscape that comes from a cyclopean bending. The images of Picasso's works bend, telescope and collide. The brilliant works take their meaning from this telescoping and juxtaposition: Picasso worked not in a linear way, but by going back and forth, by inter-related principles. Each "experiment" he created does not exist specifically as such but rather in relation to a general and gargantuan corpus. The scenography I created is an organic, thrilling disruption. The first thing to remember is that Picasso was an ogre, whose work is deeply driven, carnal, irrigated by sex and death. The very principle of the exhibition "Imagine Picasso" is perhaps, from a sensory point of view, pictorial and metaphysical, based on the notion of orgy.

RUDY RICCIOTTI

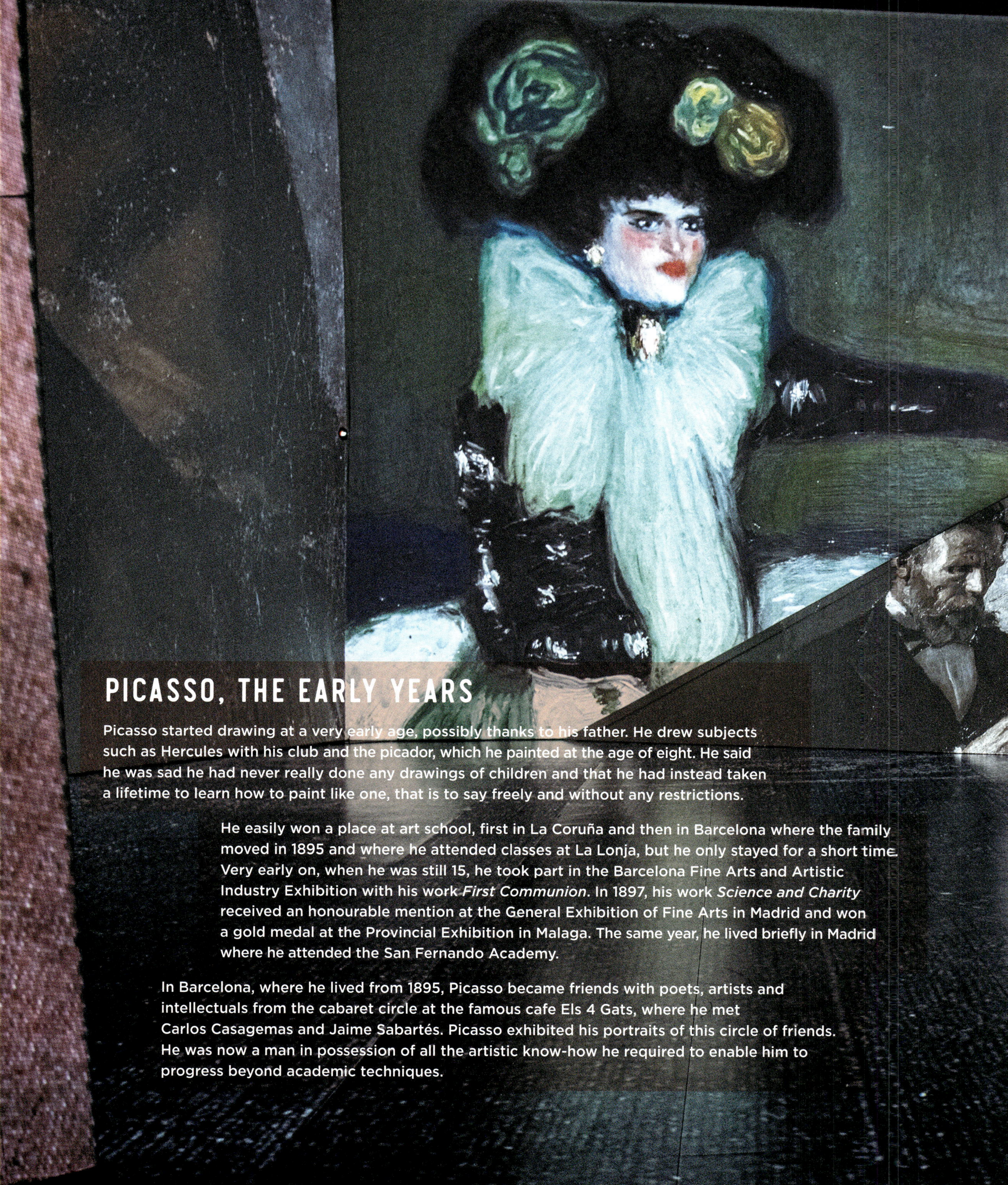

PICASSO, THE EARLY YEARS

Picasso started drawing at a very early age, possibly thanks to his father. He drew subjects such as Hercules with his club and the picador, which he painted at the age of eight. He said he was sad he had never really done any drawings of children and that he had instead taken a lifetime to learn how to paint like one, that is to say freely and without any restrictions.

He easily won a place at art school, first in La Coruña and then in Barcelona where the family moved in 1895 and where he attended classes at La Lonja, but he only stayed for a short time. Very early on, when he was still 15, he took part in the Barcelona Fine Arts and Artistic Industry Exhibition with his work *First Communion*. In 1897, his work *Science and Charity* received an honourable mention at the General Exhibition of Fine Arts in Madrid and won a gold medal at the Provincial Exhibition in Malaga. The same year, he lived briefly in Madrid where he attended the San Fernando Academy.

In Barcelona, where he lived from 1895, Picasso became friends with poets, artists and intellectuals from the cabaret circle at the famous cafe Els 4 Gats, where he met Carlos Casagemas and Jaime Sabartés. Picasso exhibited his portraits of this circle of friends. He was now a man in possession of all the artistic know-how he required to enable him to progress beyond academic techniques.

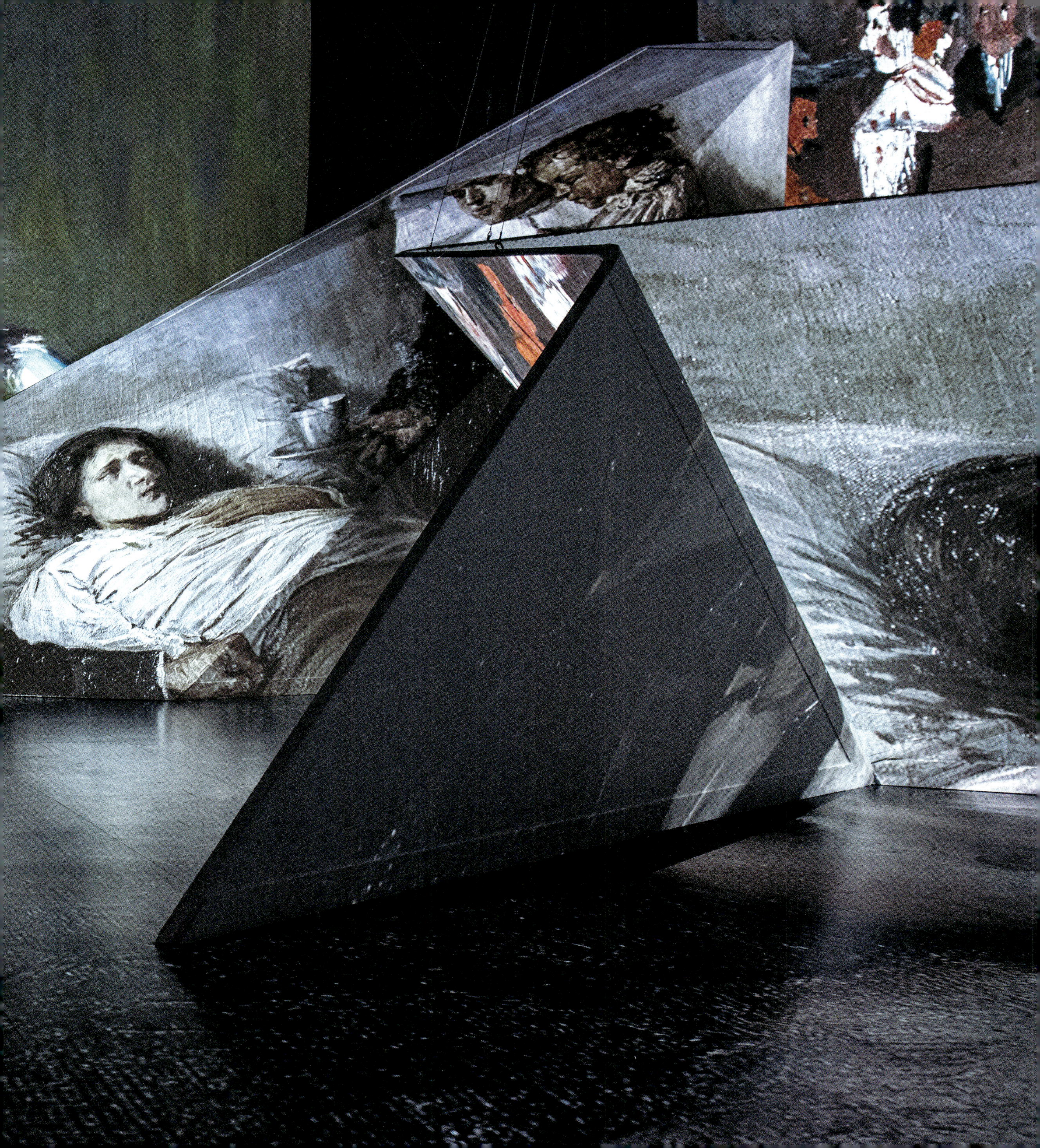

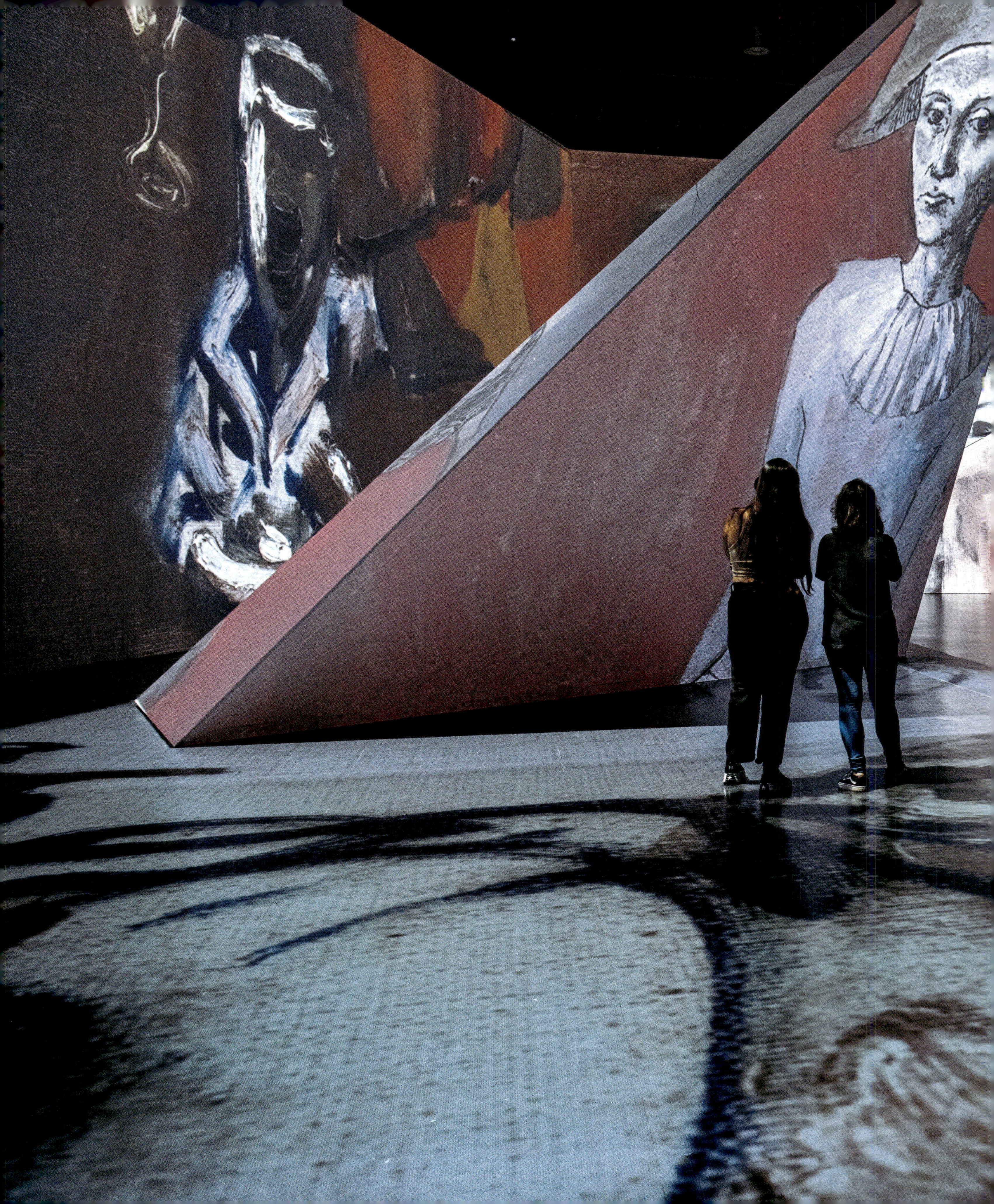

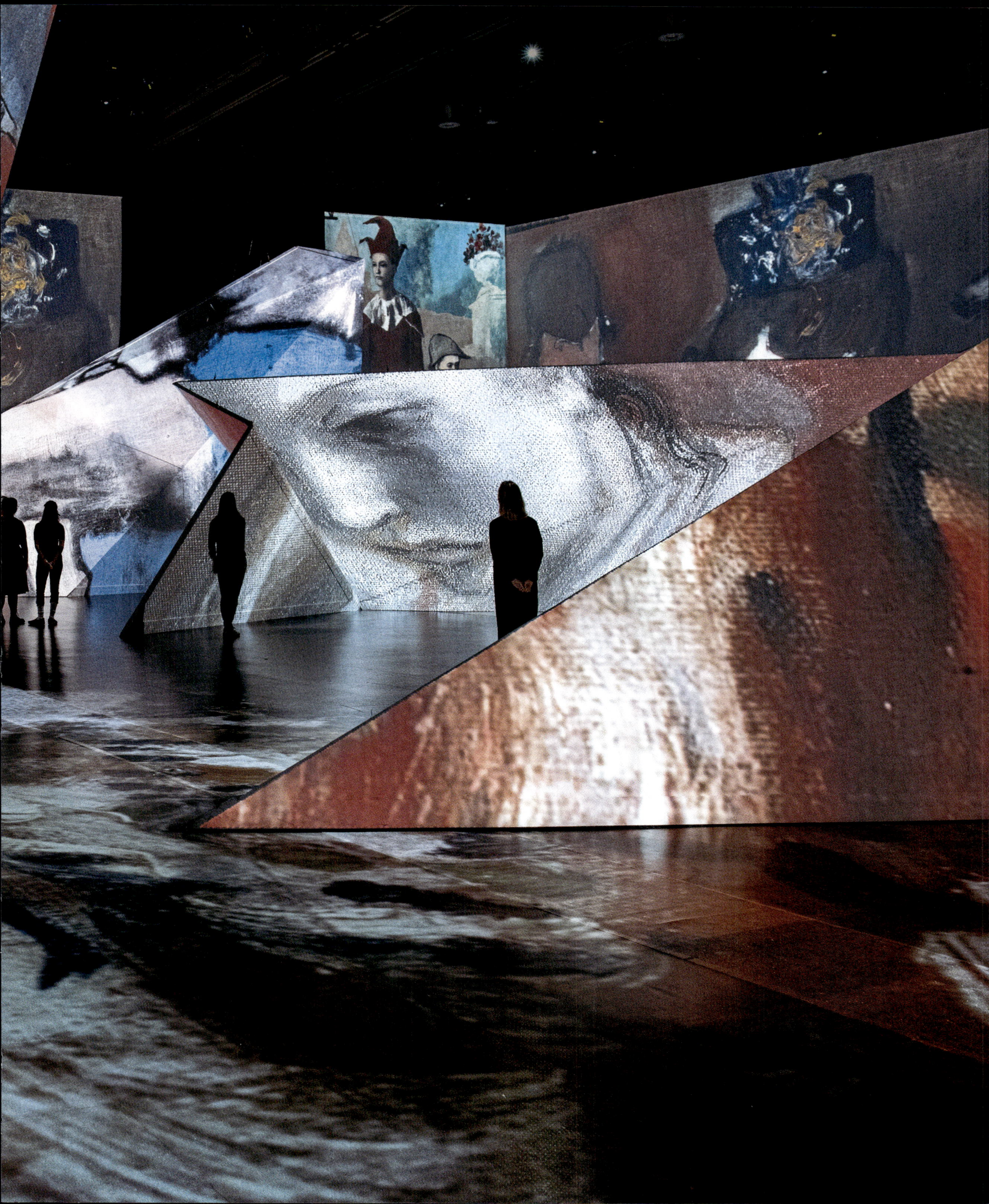

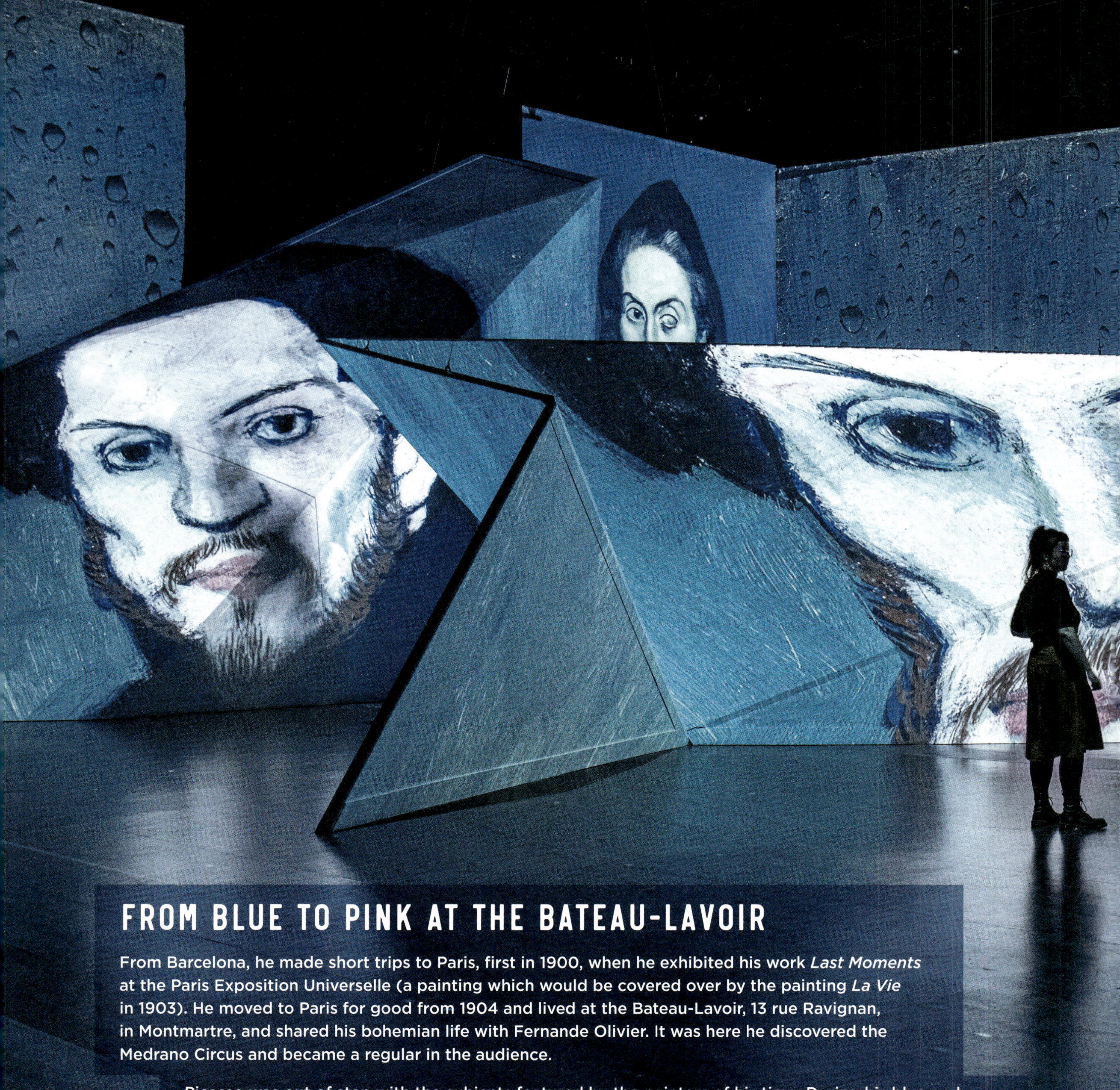

FROM BLUE TO PINK AT THE BATEAU-LAVOIR

From Barcelona, he made short trips to Paris, first in 1900, when he exhibited his work *Last Moments* at the Paris Exposition Universelle (a painting which would be covered over by the painting *La Vie* in 1903). He moved to Paris for good from 1904 and lived at the Bateau-Lavoir, 13 rue Ravignan, in Montmartre, and shared his bohemian life with Fernande Olivier. It was here he discovered the Medrano Circus and became a regular in the audience.

Picasso was out of step with the subjects featured by the painters of his time. During his blue and pink periods, he turned his gaze on human destiny, on those who live on the margins of society, women on their own, old men and the blind. The world of the circus and the landscapes of Gosol were painted in lighter tones of pink. His treatment of faces and space was already hinting at the great change that occurred with *Les demoiselles d'Avignon* (1907). This was a revolutionary moment, the creation of an entirely new modern perspective and this flagship work paved the way for cubism.

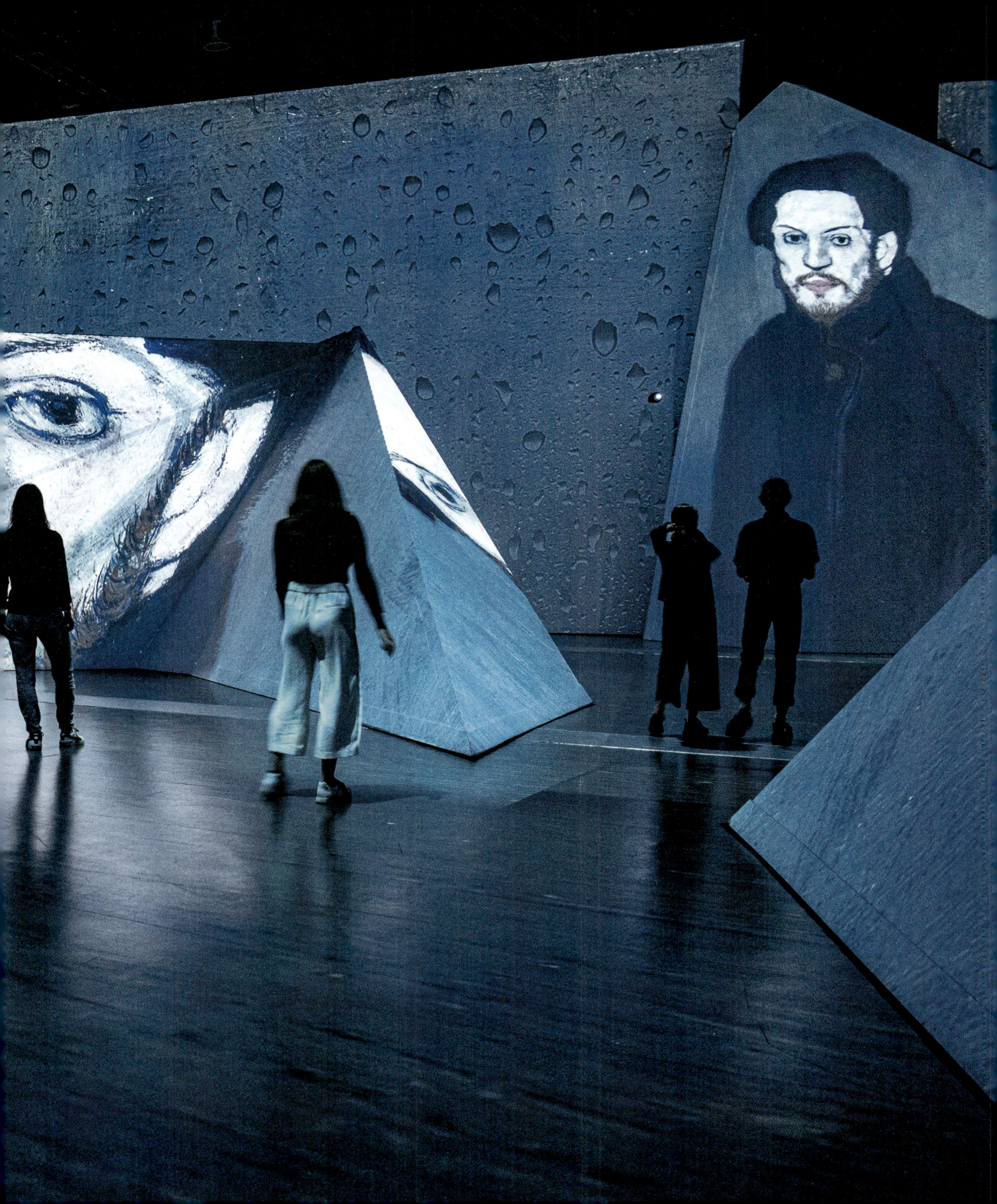

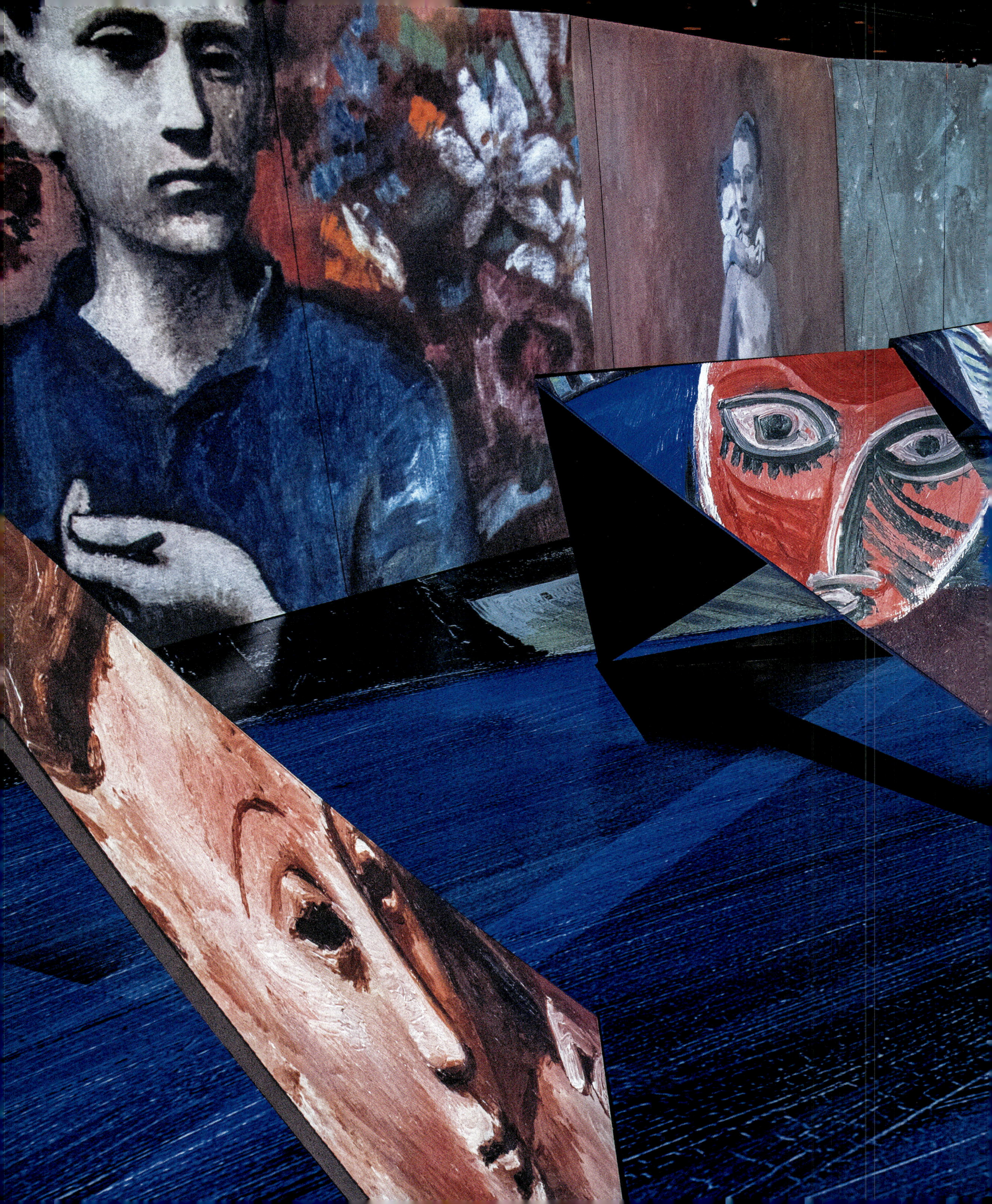

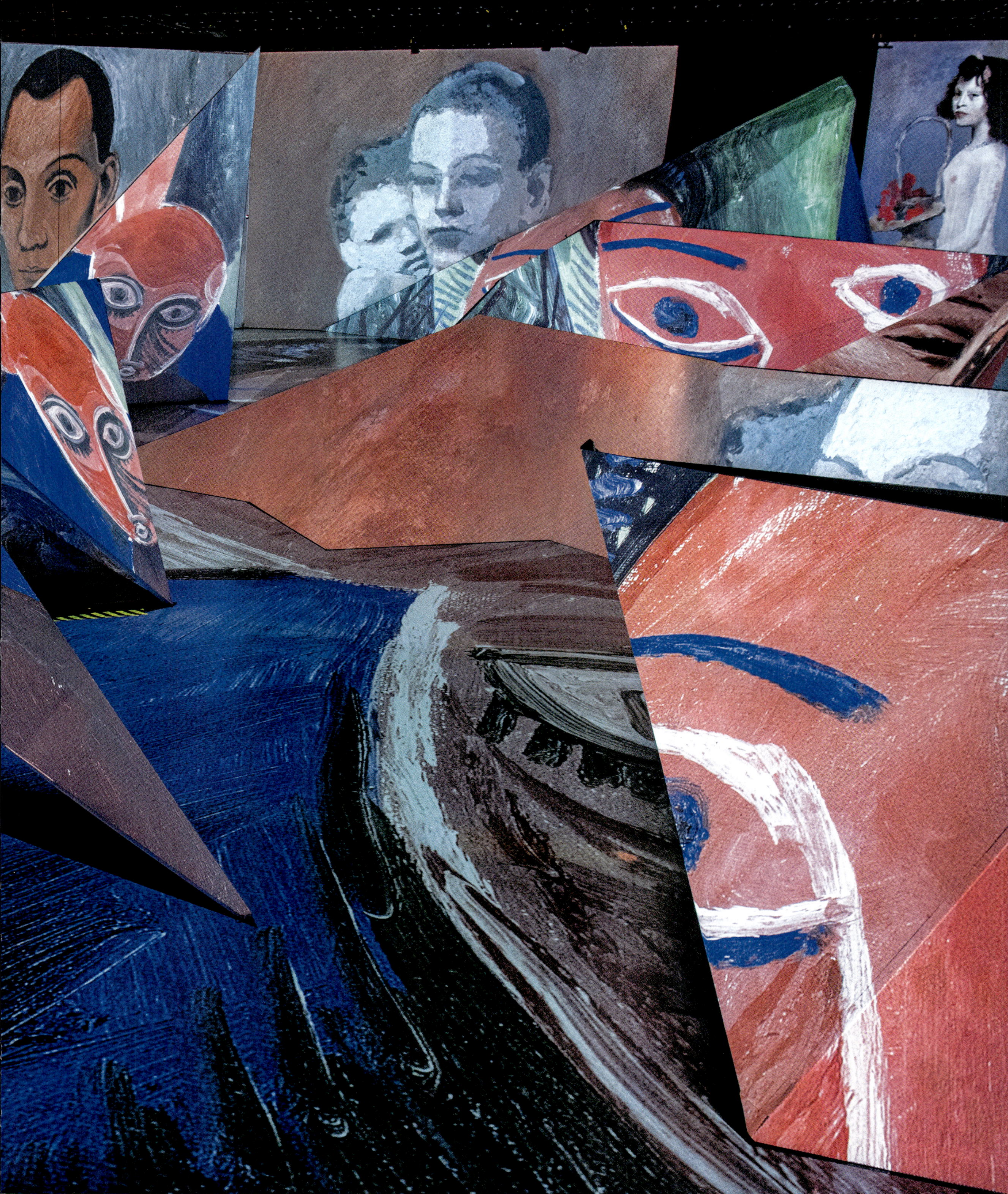

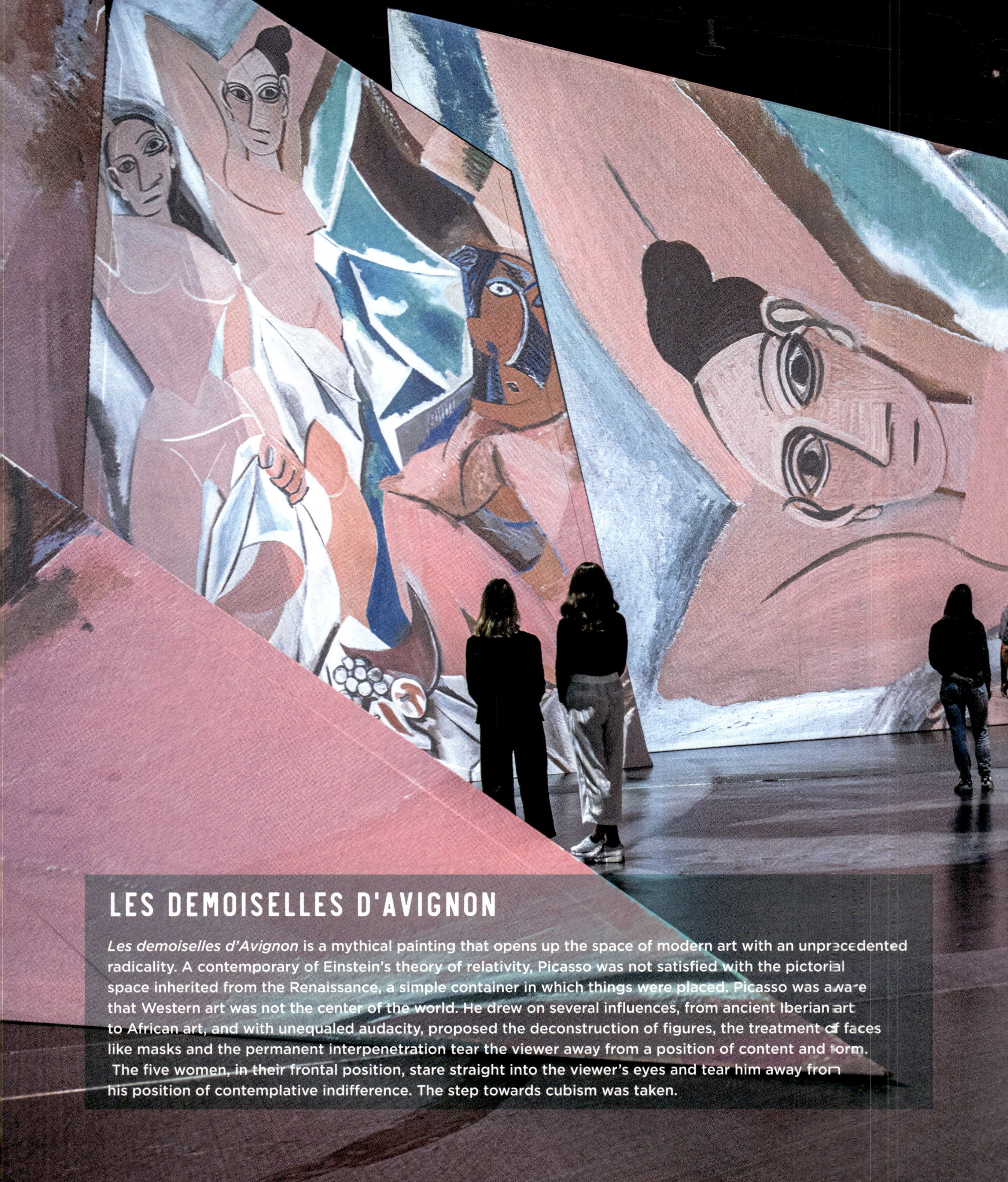

LES DEMOISELLES D'AVIGNON

Les demoiselles d'Avignon is a mythical painting that opens up the space of modern art with an unprecedented radicality. A contemporary of Einstein's theory of relativity, Picasso was not satisfied with the pictorial space inherited from the Renaissance, a simple container in which things were placed. Picasso was aware that Western art was not the center of the world. He drew on several influences, from ancient Iberian art to African art, and with unequaled audacity, proposed the deconstruction of figures, the treatment of faces like masks and the permanent interpenetration tear the viewer away from a position of content and form. The five women, in their frontal position, stare straight into the viewer's eyes and tear him away from his position of contemplative indifference. The step towards cubism was taken.

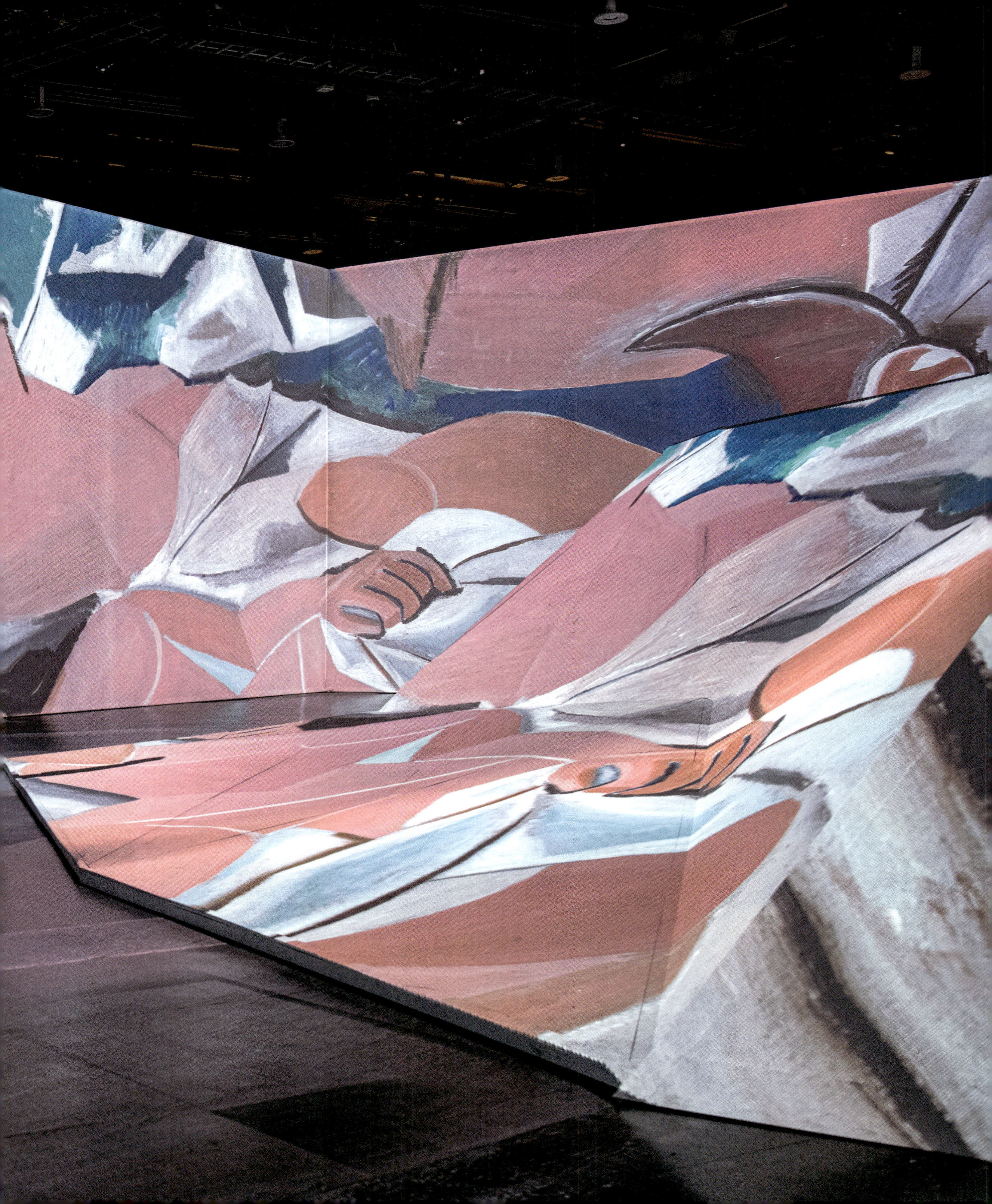

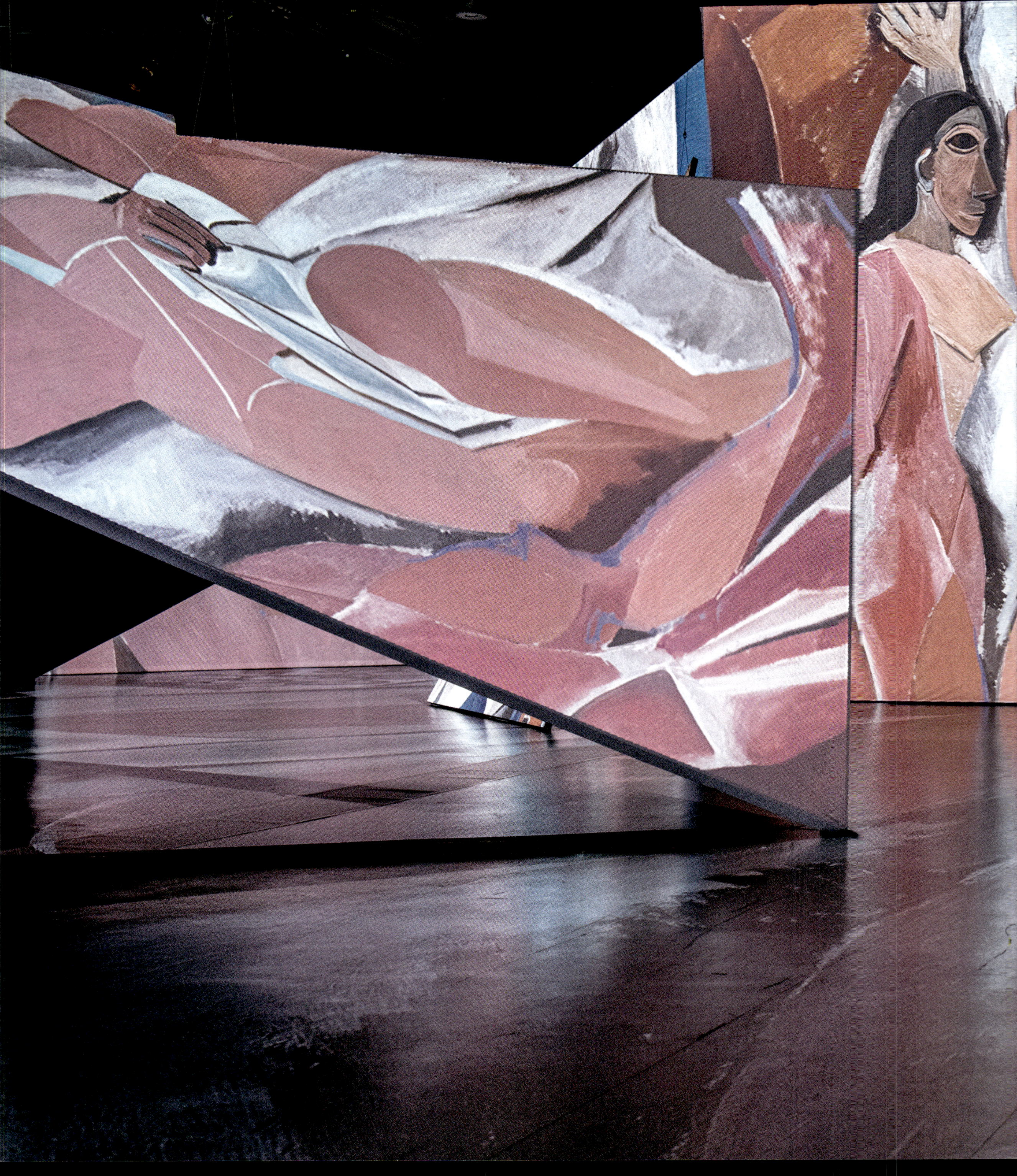

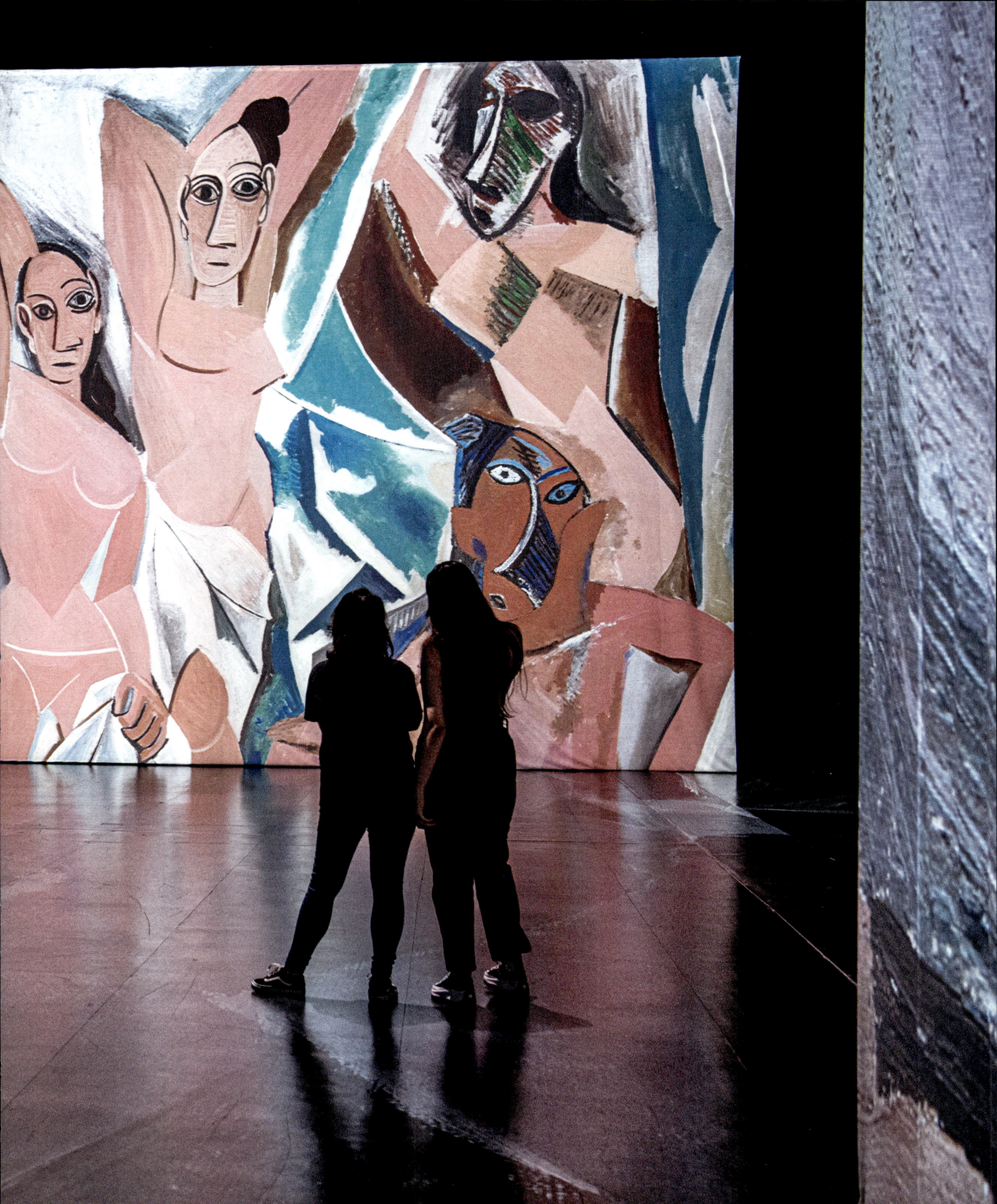

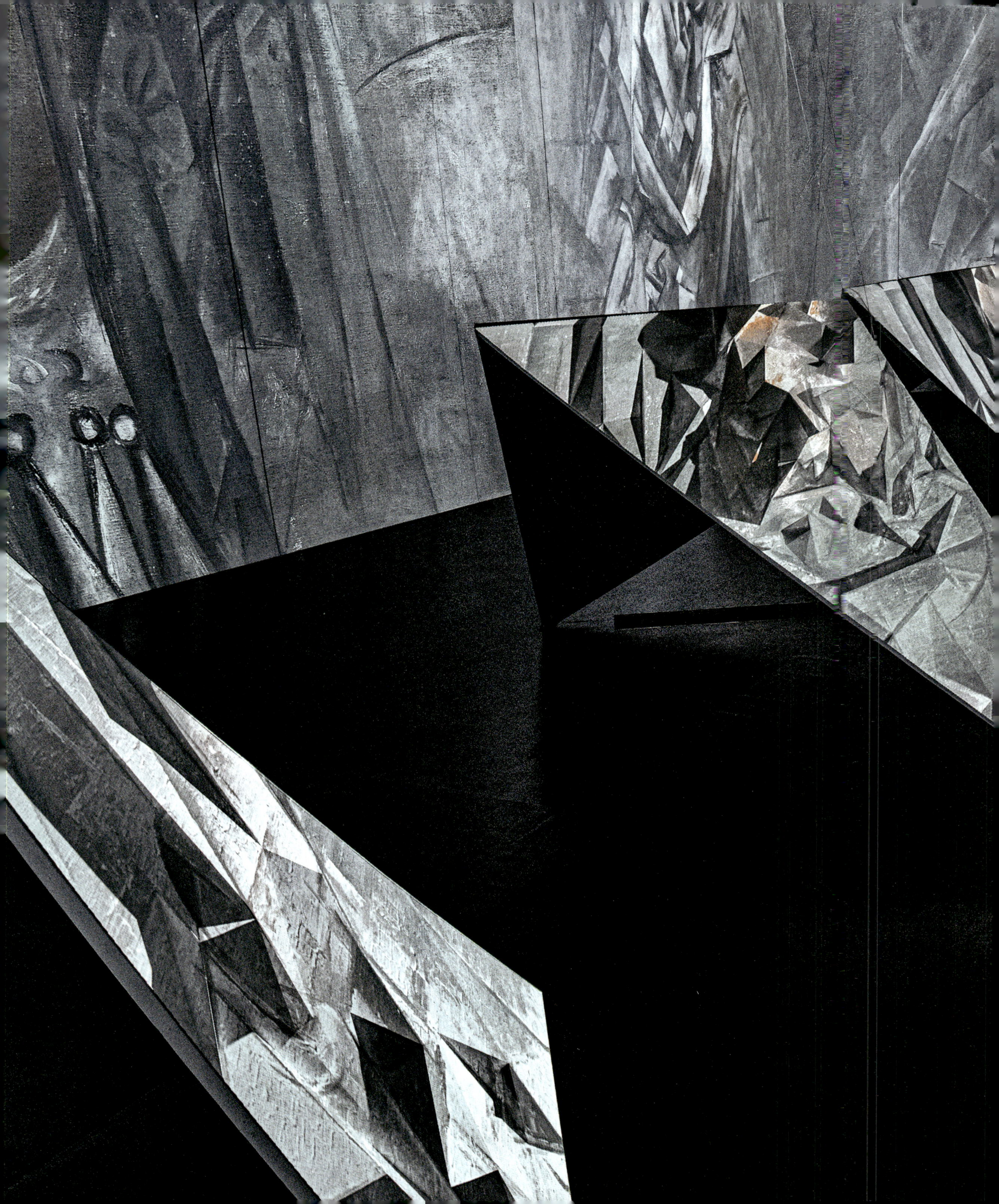

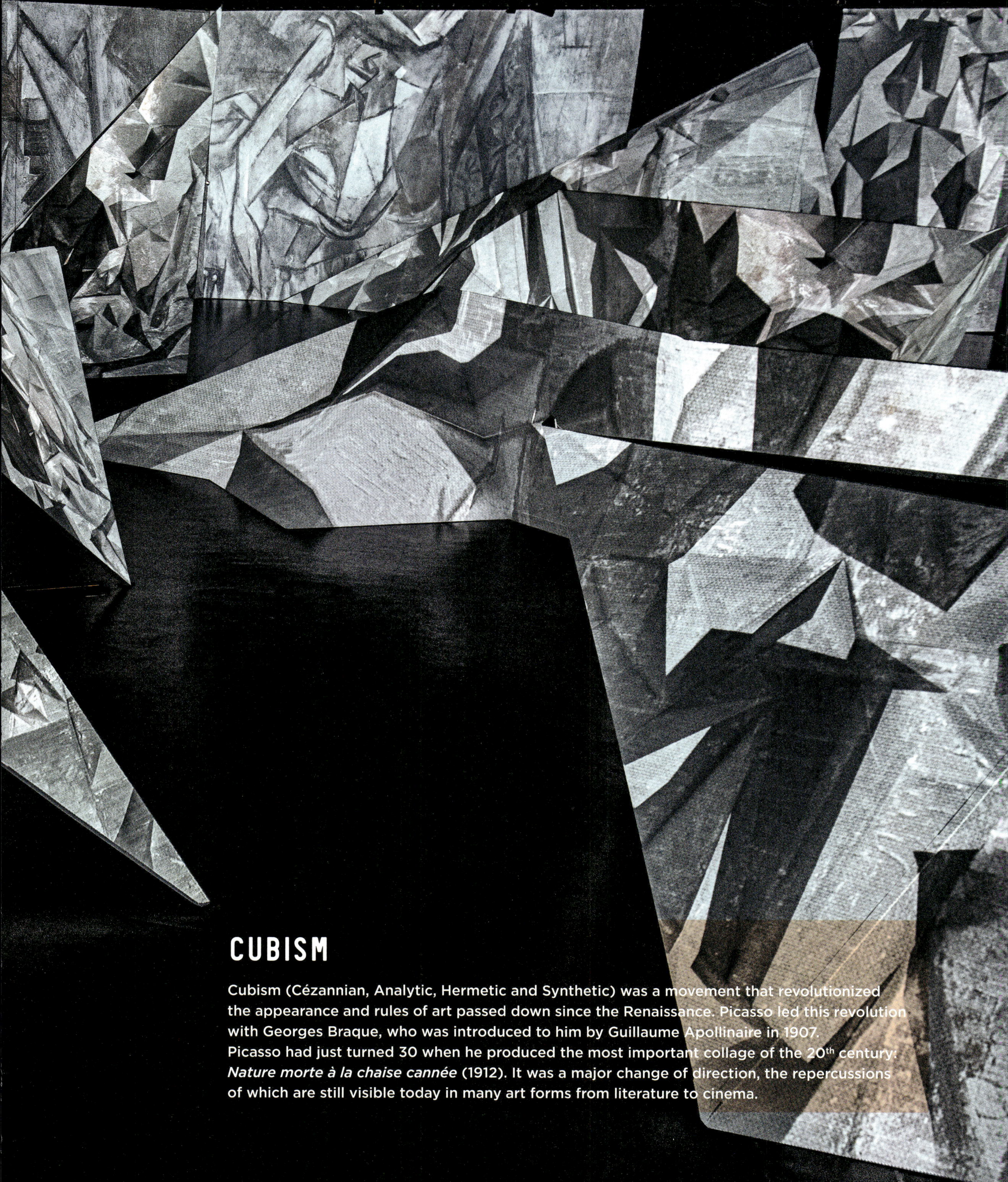

CUBISM

Cubism (Cézannian, Analytic, Hermetic and Synthetic) was a movement that revolutionized the appearance and rules of art passed down since the Renaissance. Picasso led this revolution with Georges Braque, who was introduced to him by Guillaume Apollinaire in 1907.
Picasso had just turned 30 when he produced the most important collage of the 20th century: *Nature morte à la chaise cannée* (1912). It was a major change of direction, the repercussions of which are still visible today in many art forms from literature to cinema.

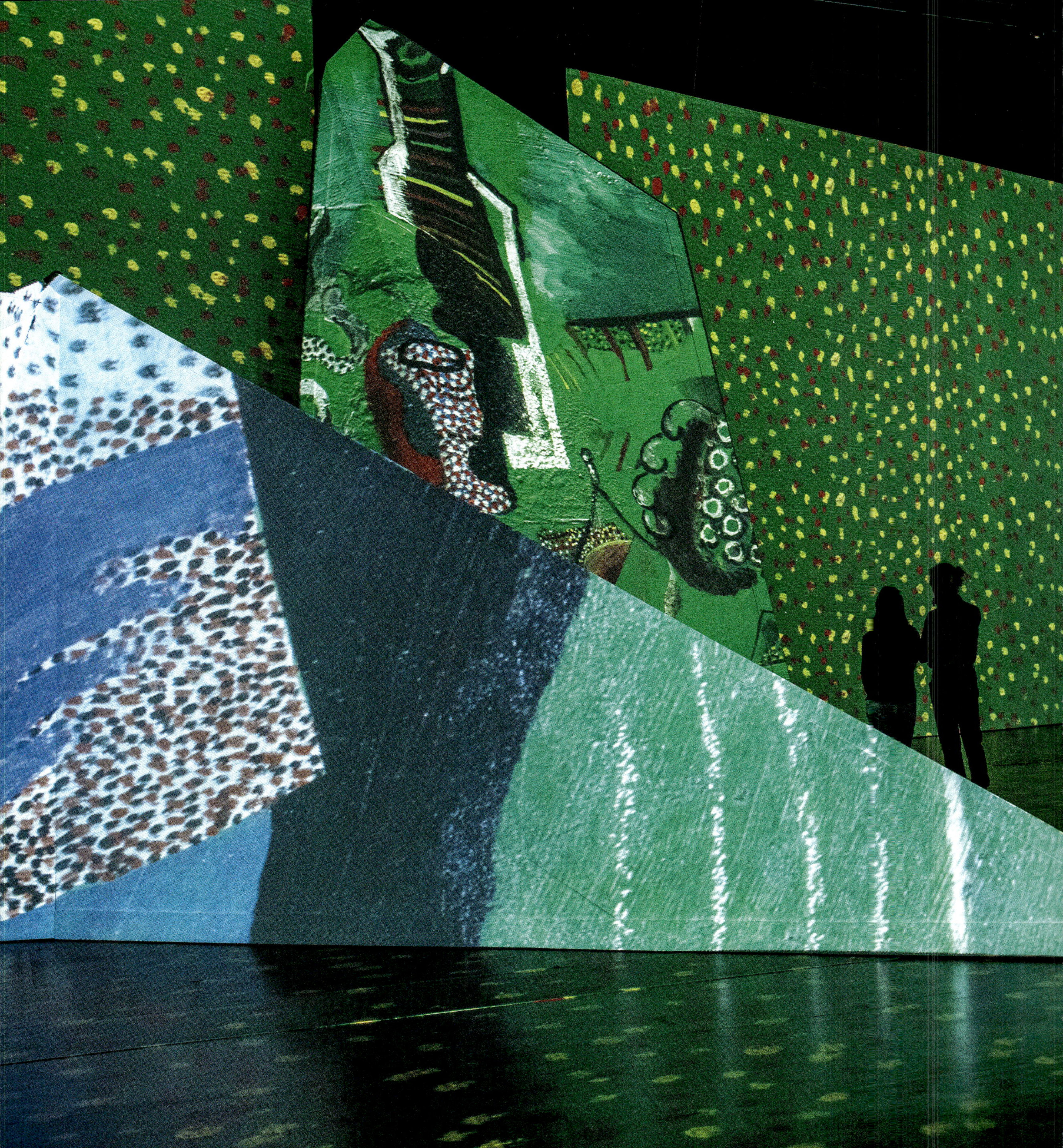

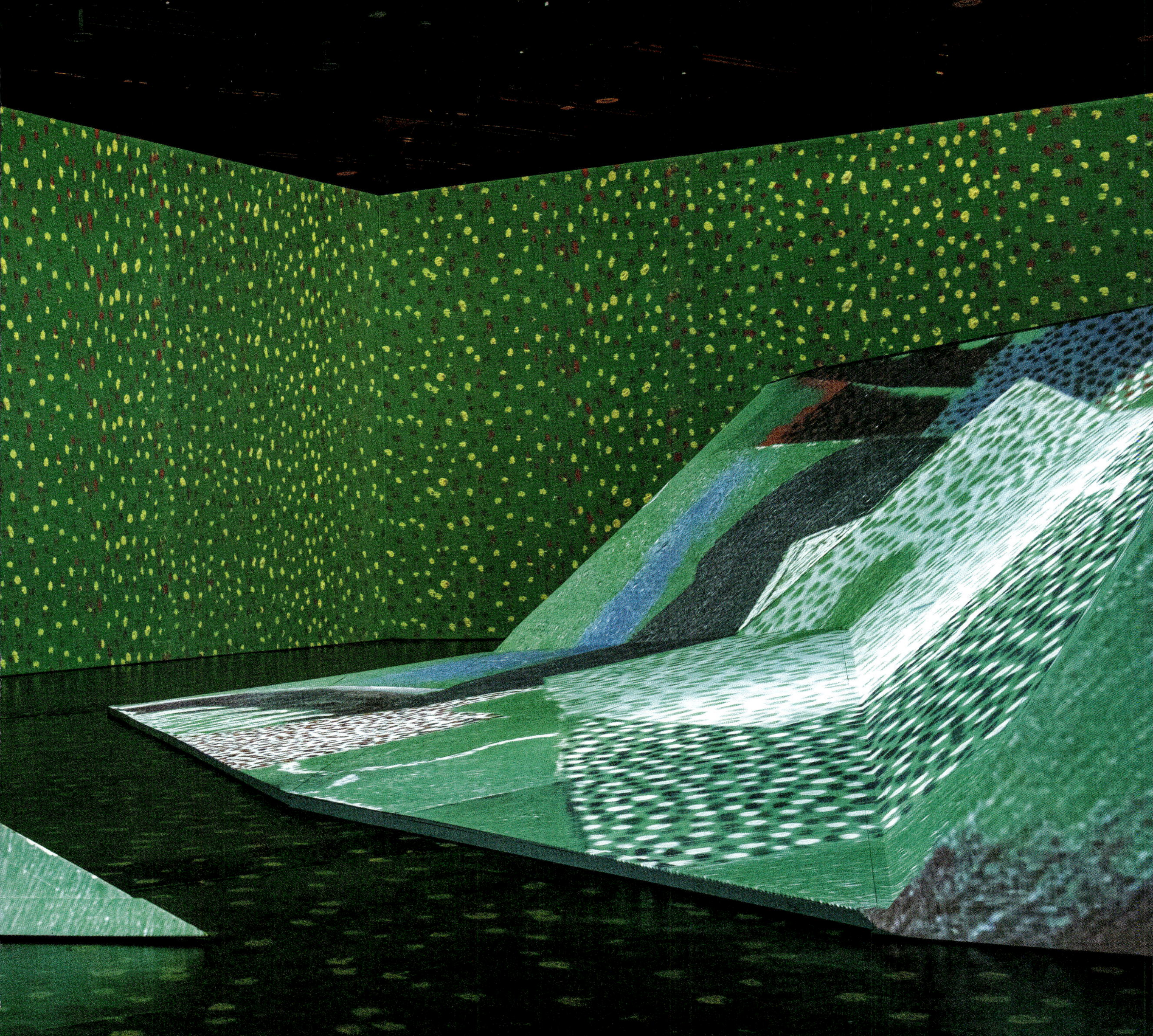

THE BALLETS RUSSES
AND THE "NEOCLASSICAL" PERIOD

From the mid-1890s to the mid-1920s, Picasso continued to combine cubism and realism, even reverting to a type of classicism. His collaboration with Serge de Diaghilev's avant-garde Ballets Russes took him to Italy, one of the few countries he traveled to. In the ballet *Parade* (1917), a flagship work in his collaboration with the most famous ballet company of the time, Picasso combined all the styles that were important to him without worrying about classifications. His art then grew to encompass the stage sets, costumes and stage curtain.

It was here that he met the ballerina Olga Khokhlova who became his wife and of whom he painted numerous portraits where he experimented with realism, a far cry from the cubism that he continued to explore in other paintings. He also painted some superb portraits of his first son Paulo in Harlequin, Pierrot, or on a donkey. He moved into a bourgeois apartment on Rue de la Boétie, not far from his gallery owner Rosenberg, who was happy to see that the great Picasso could also produce works of much greater realism and which were more appealing to buyers. Picasso had become a great artist in a comfortable position. In 1932 he held his first major retrospective in Zurich, which he organised himself, choosing the works to be included and how they were hung.

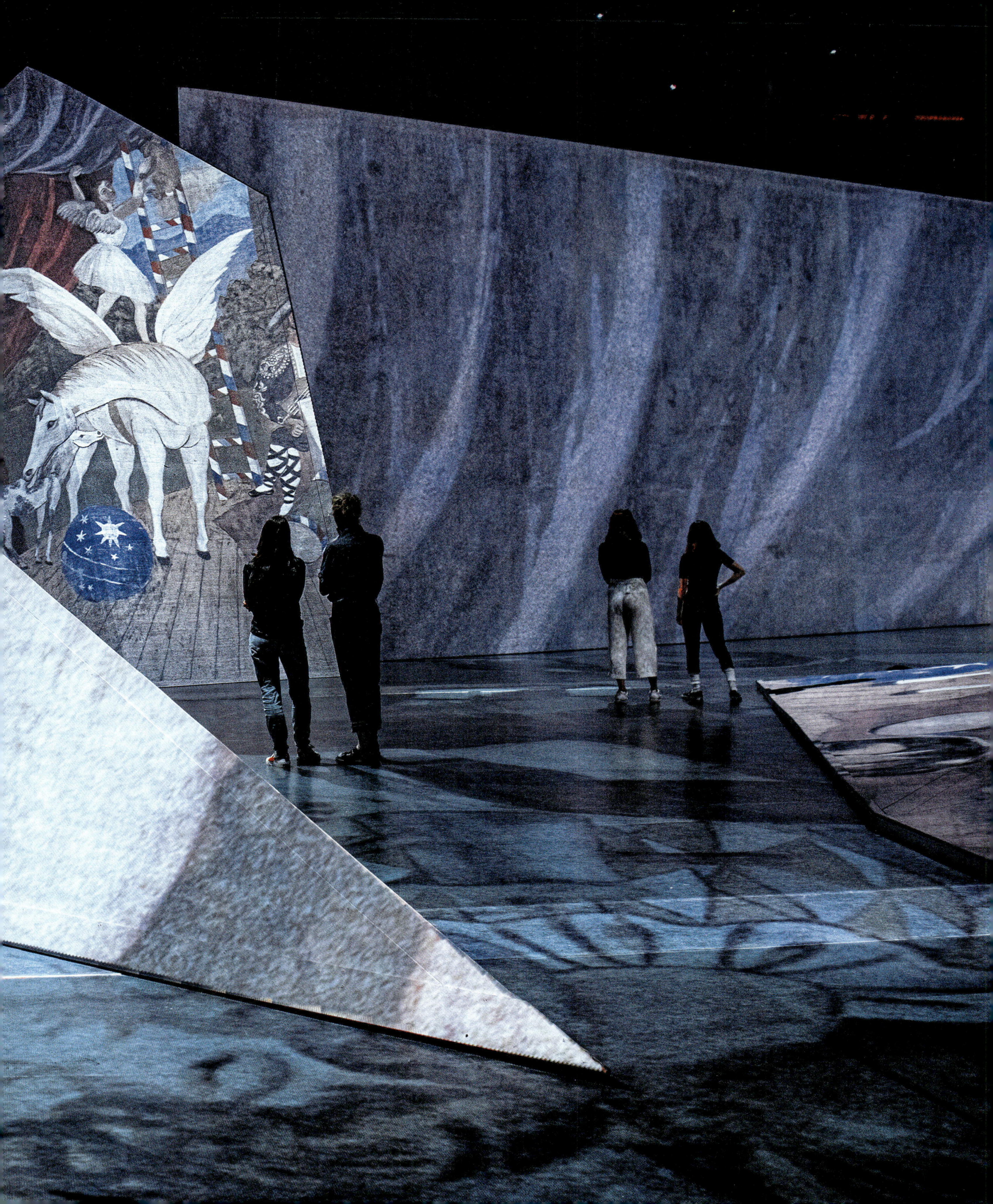

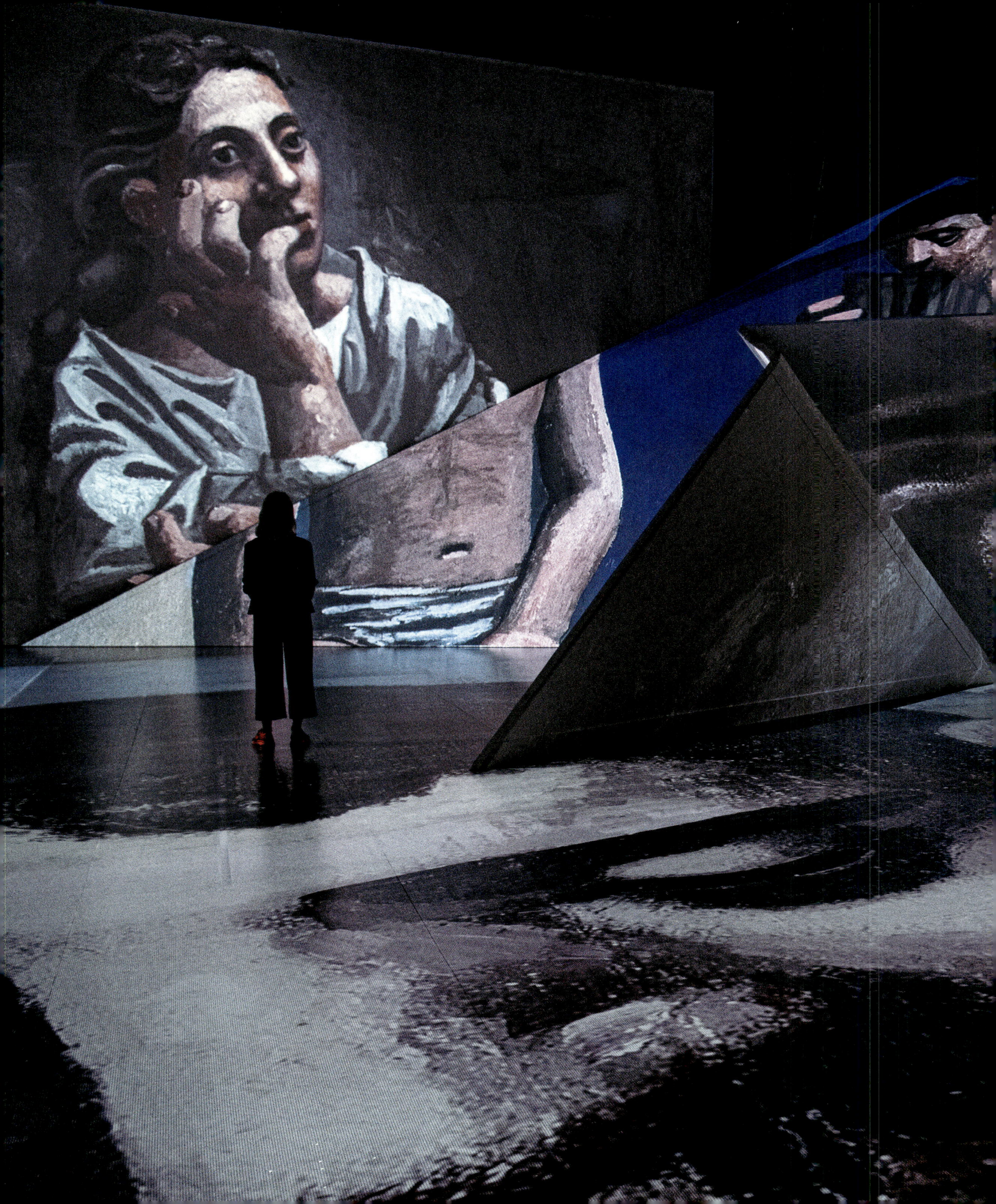

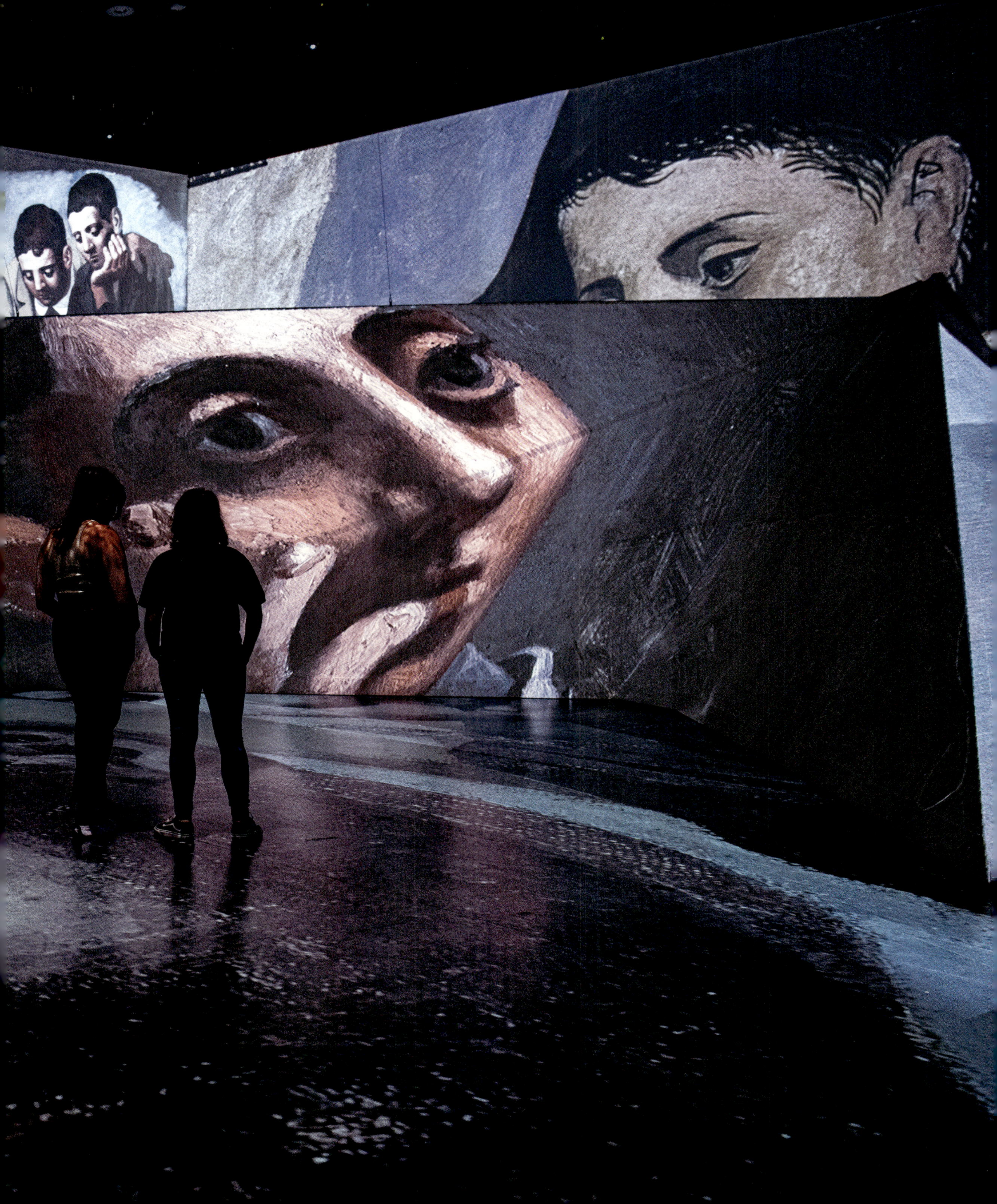

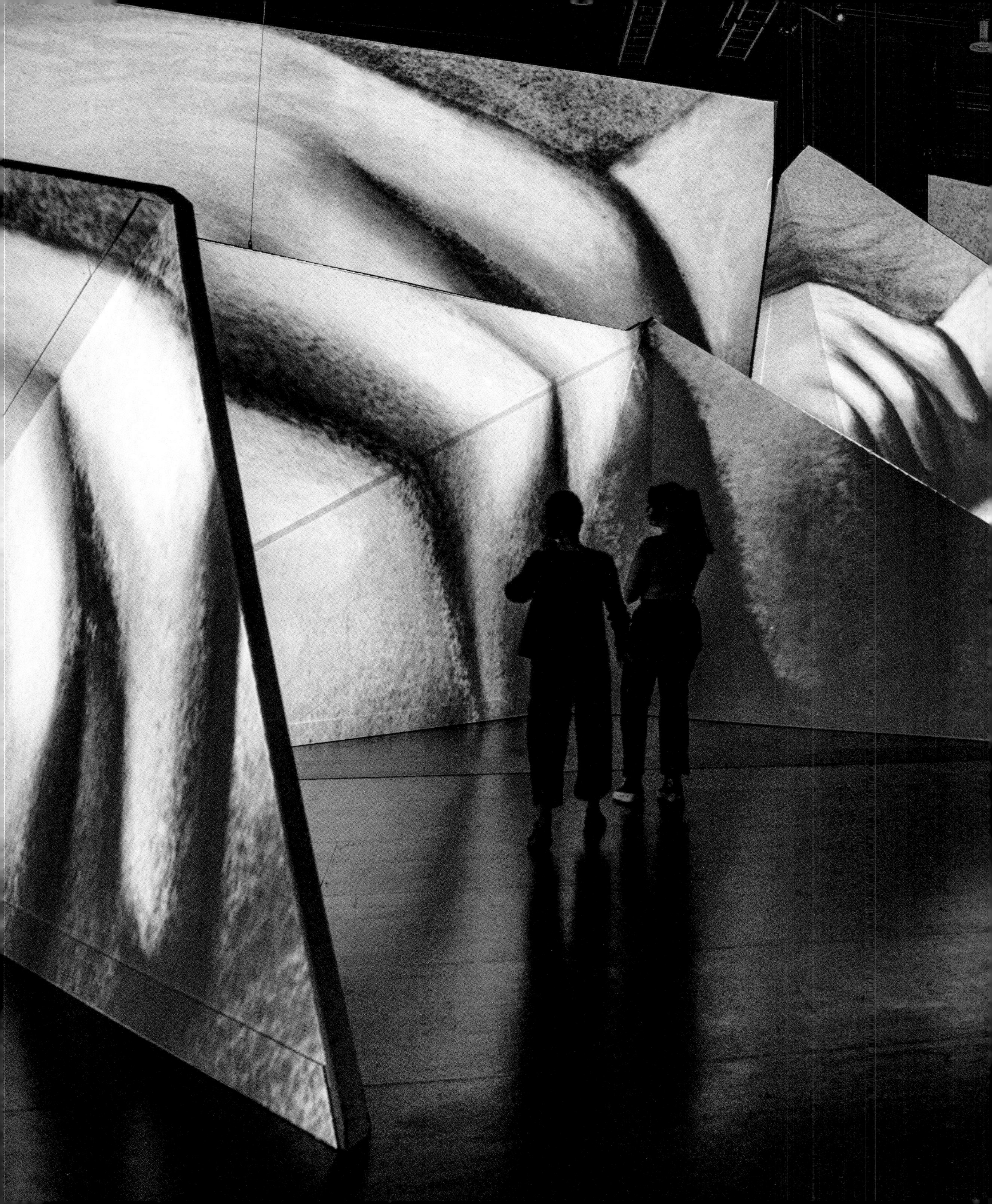

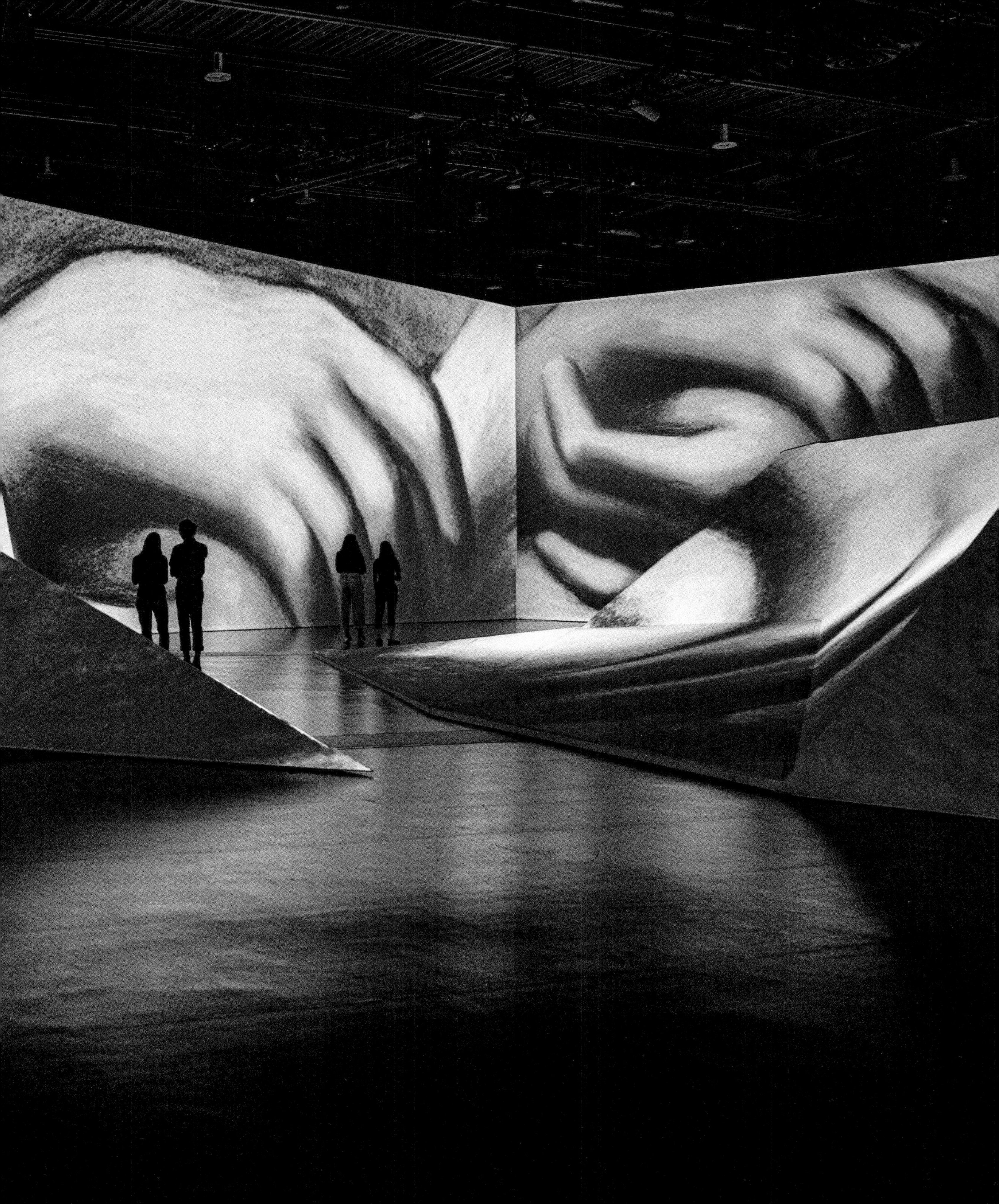

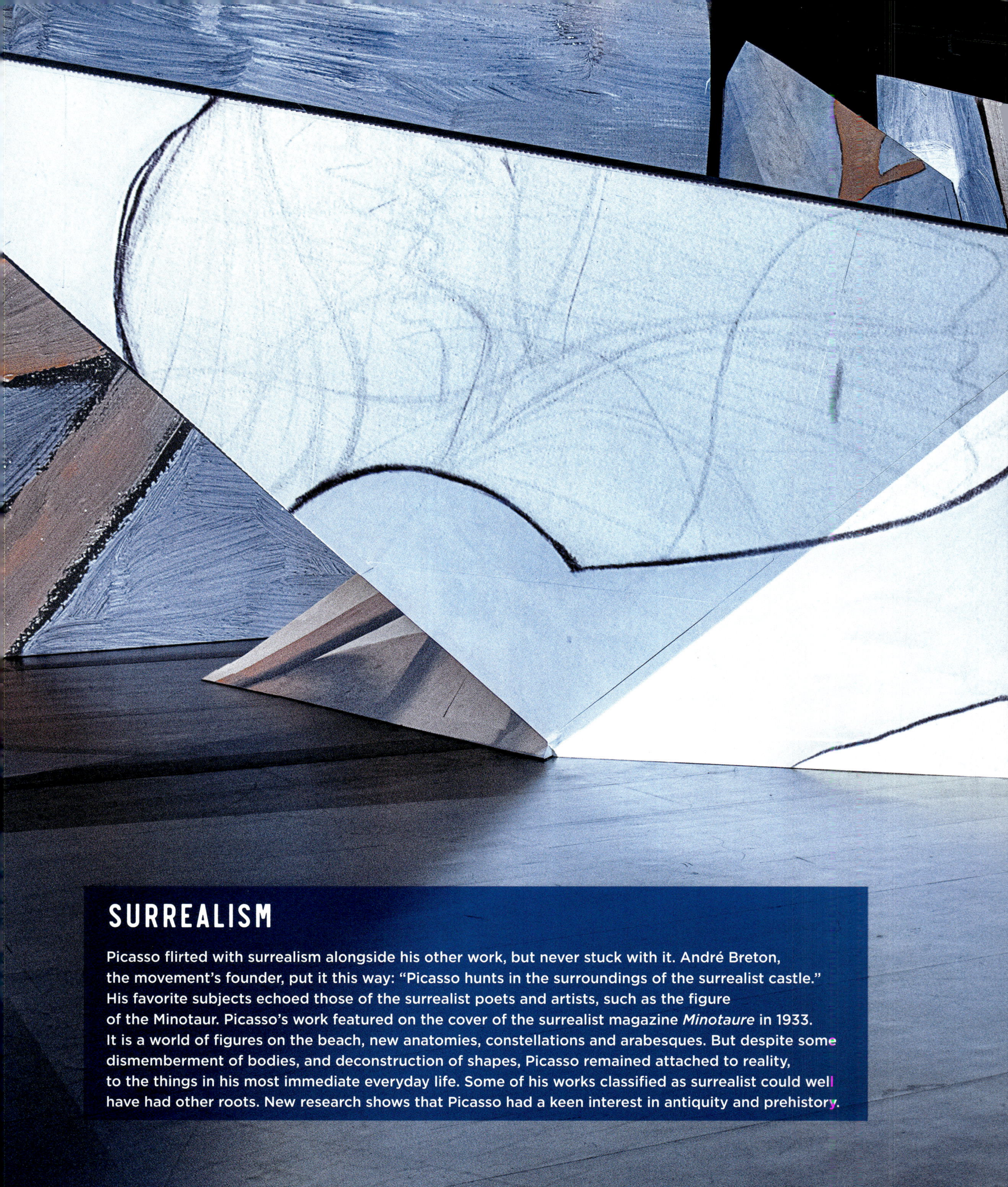

SURREALISM

Picasso flirted with surrealism alongside his other work, but never stuck with it. André Breton, the movement's founder, put it this way: "Picasso hunts in the surroundings of the surrealist castle." His favorite subjects echoed those of the surrealist poets and artists, such as the figure of the Minotaur. Picasso's work featured on the cover of the surrealist magazine *Minotaure* in 1933. It is a world of figures on the beach, new anatomies, constellations and arabesques. But despite some dismemberment of bodies, and deconstruction of shapes, Picasso remained attached to reality, to the things in his most immediate everyday life. Some of his works classified as surrealist could well have had other roots. New research shows that Picasso had a keen interest in antiquity and prehistory.

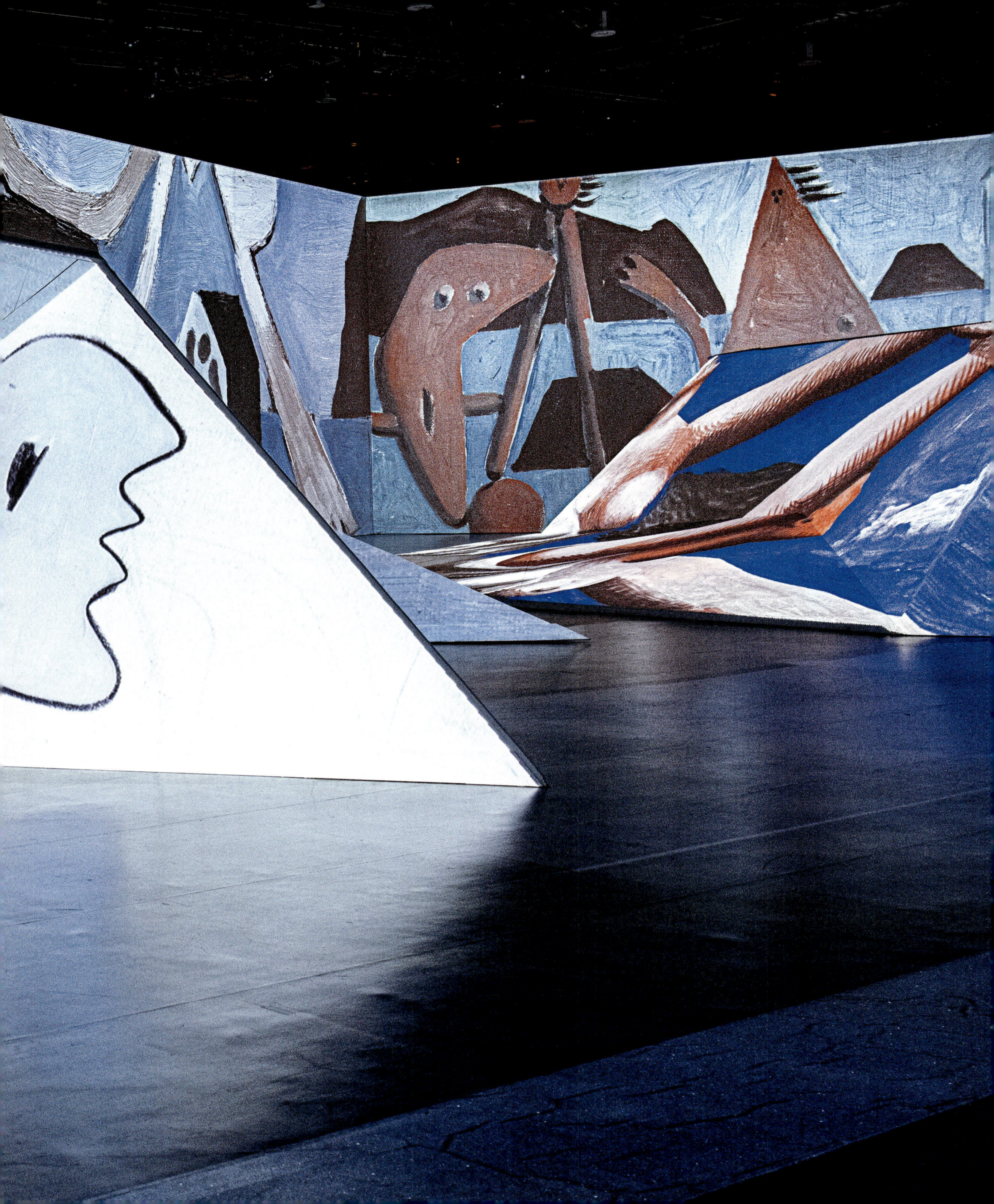

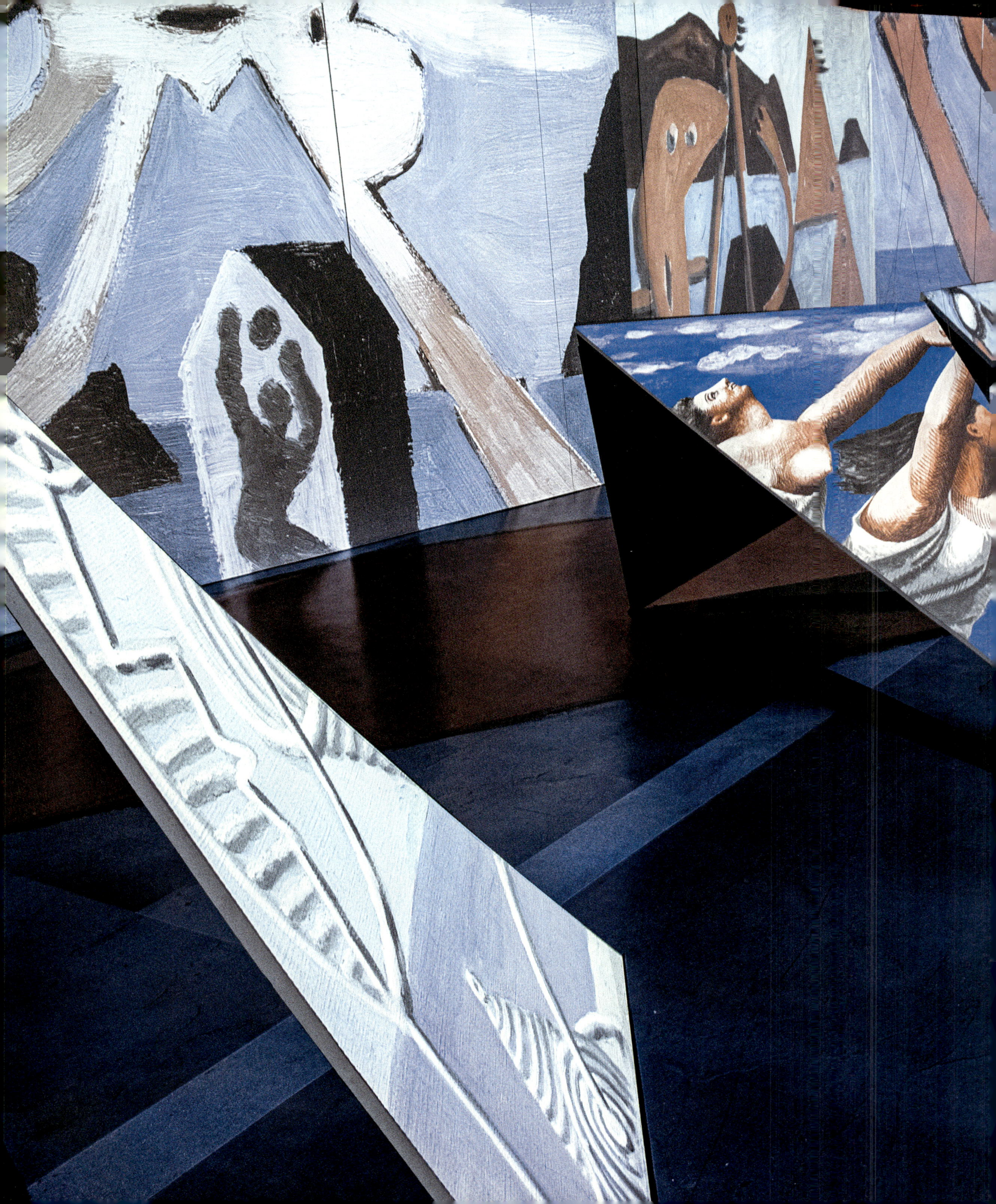

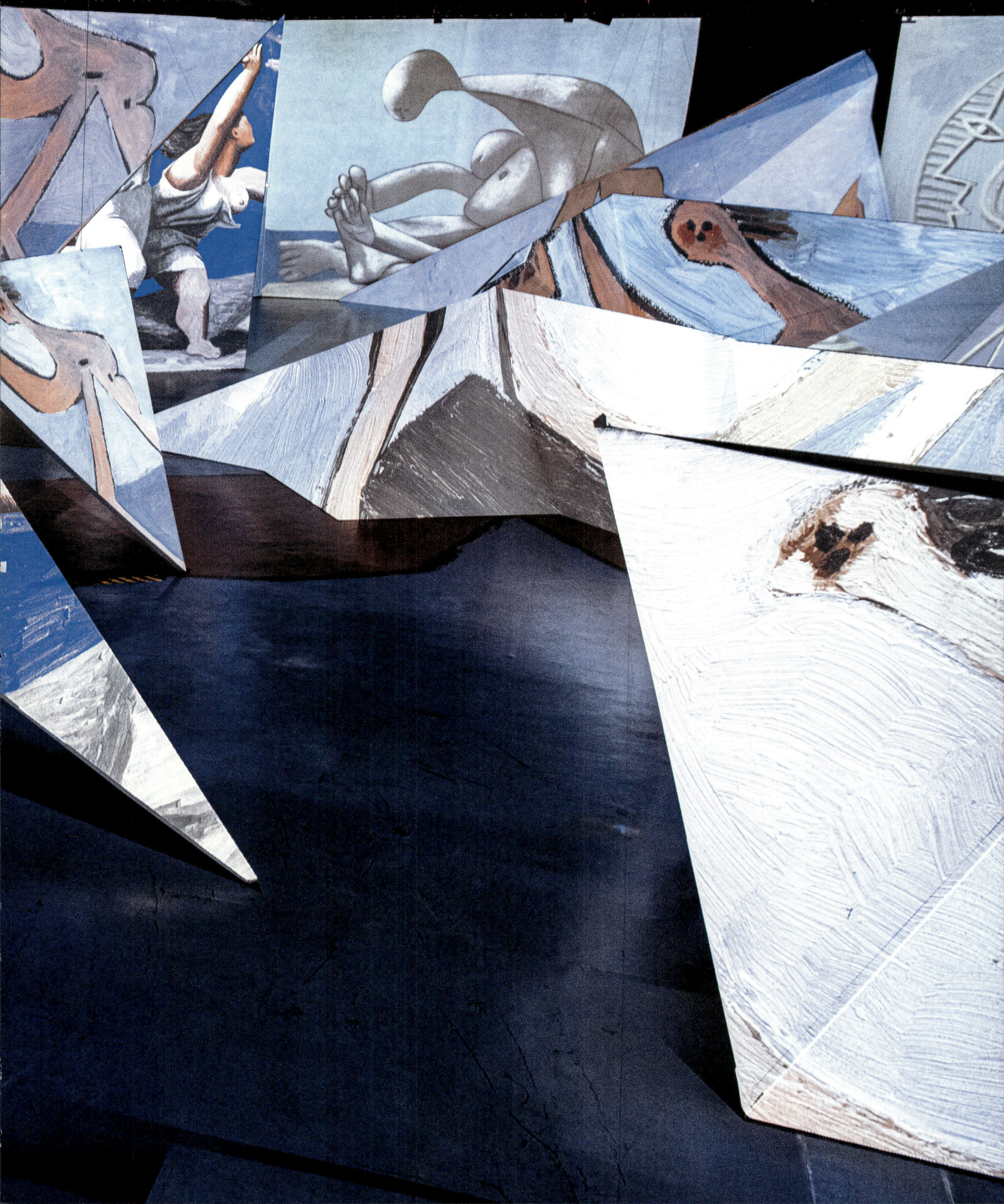

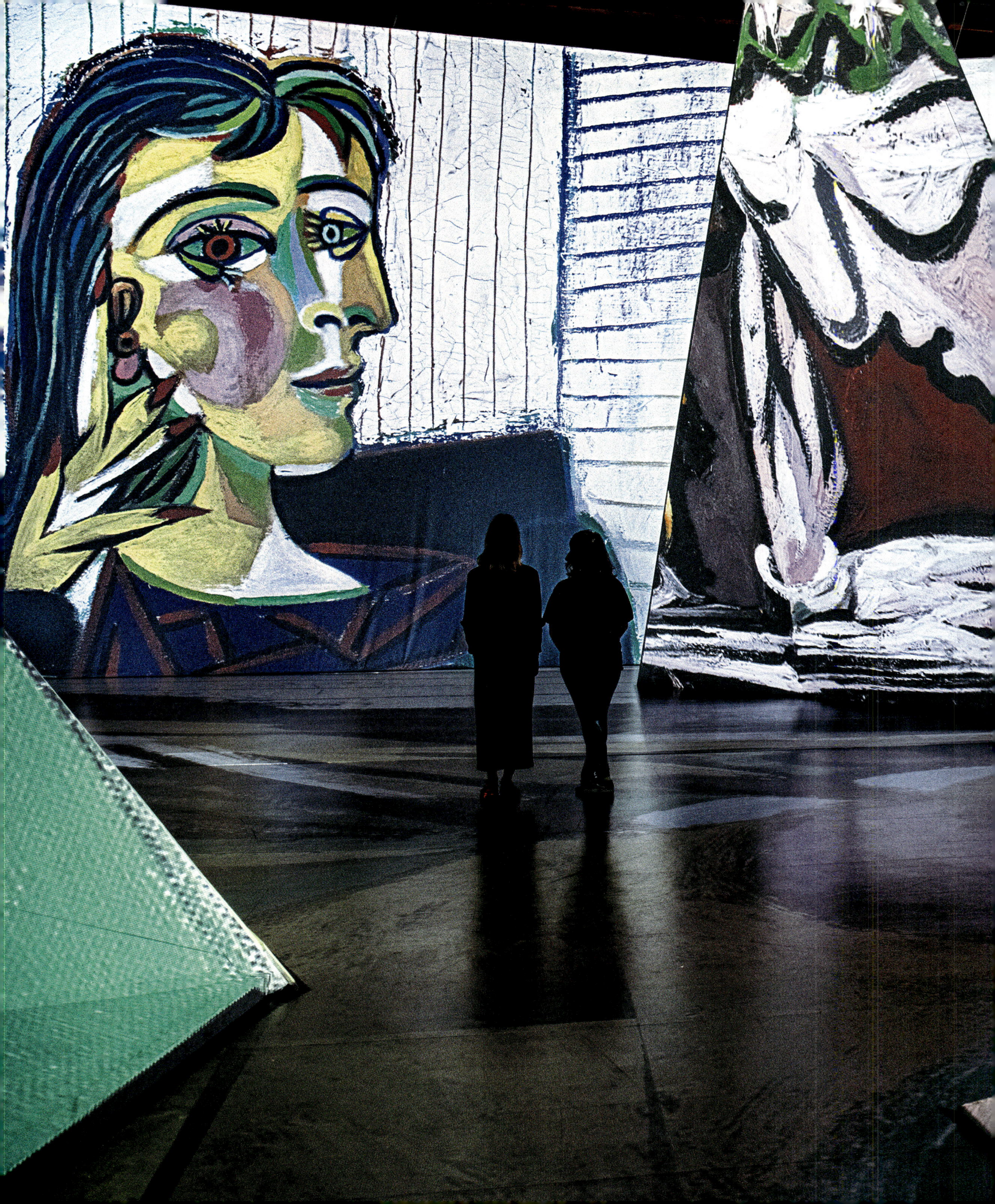

PORTRAITS OF WOMEN

Picasso represented women throughout his life: women in his family environment and women with whom he was in love. Picasso observed and scrutinized the women around him but never asked them to pose for him. Whether seated in an armchair, reclining or seen from unusual angles, women are the inspiration for Picasso's work. But a painted woman is not to be confused with the *real* woman. The latter gives him the initial vision to become, once in the picture, a fiction, and a problem of another order.

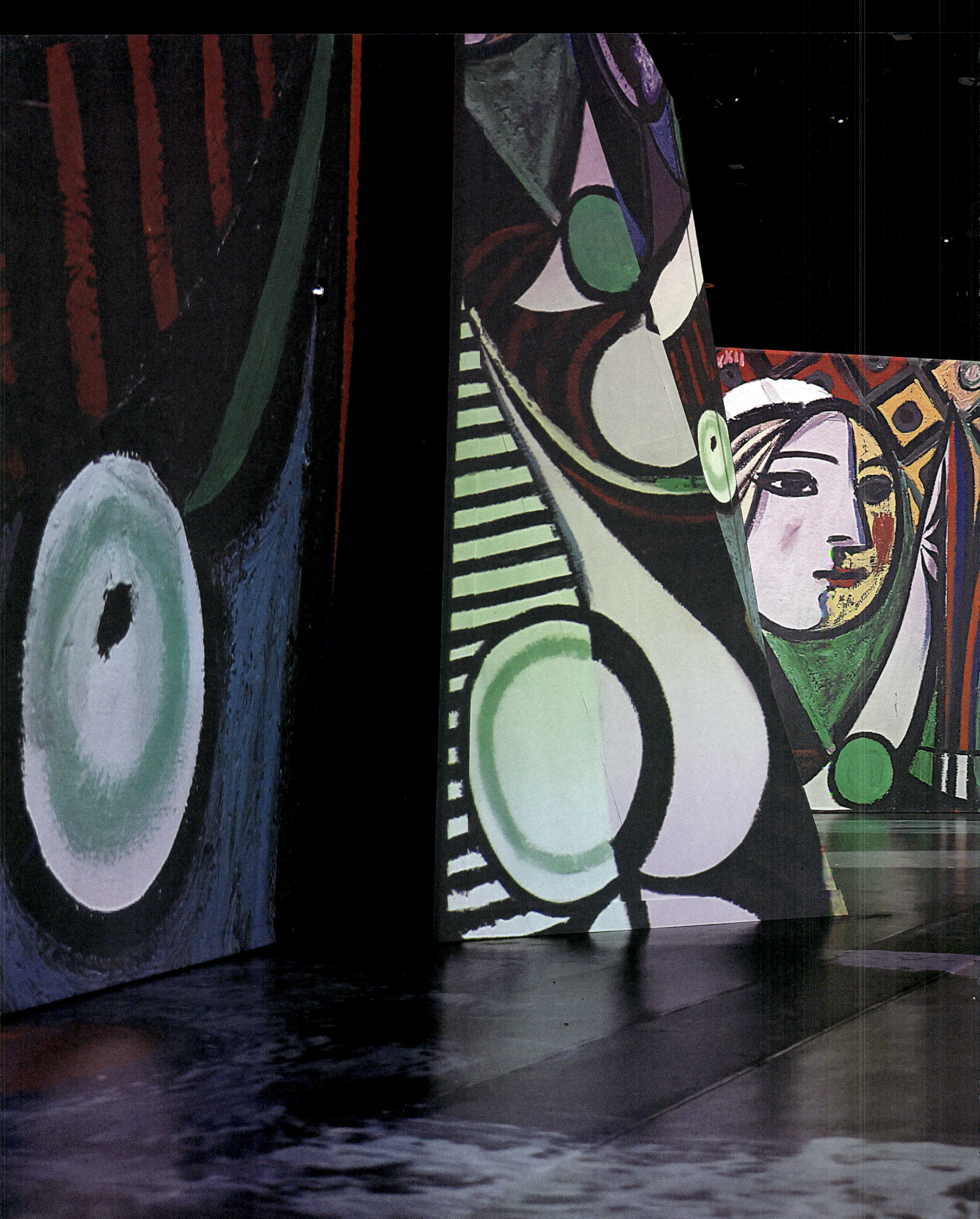

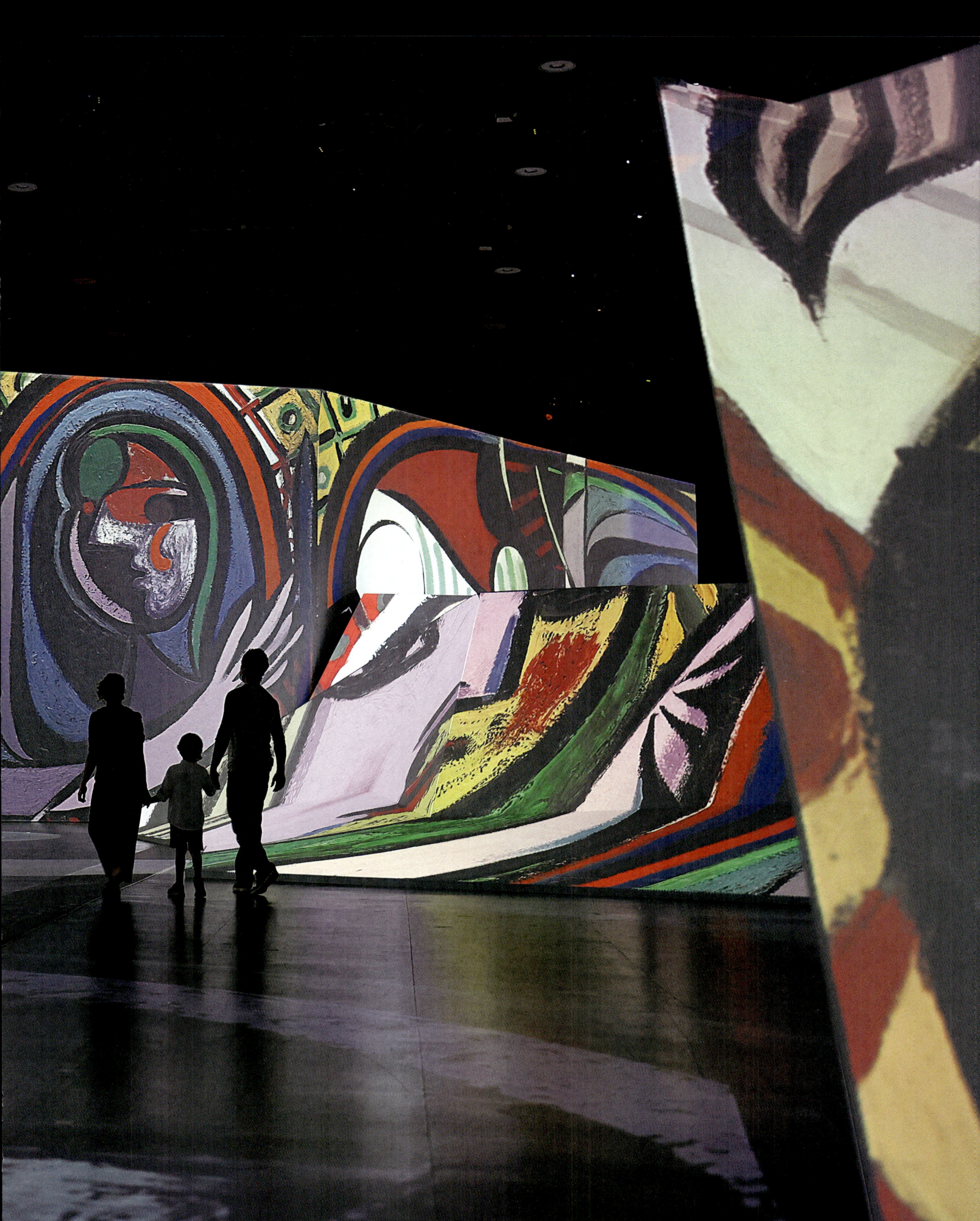

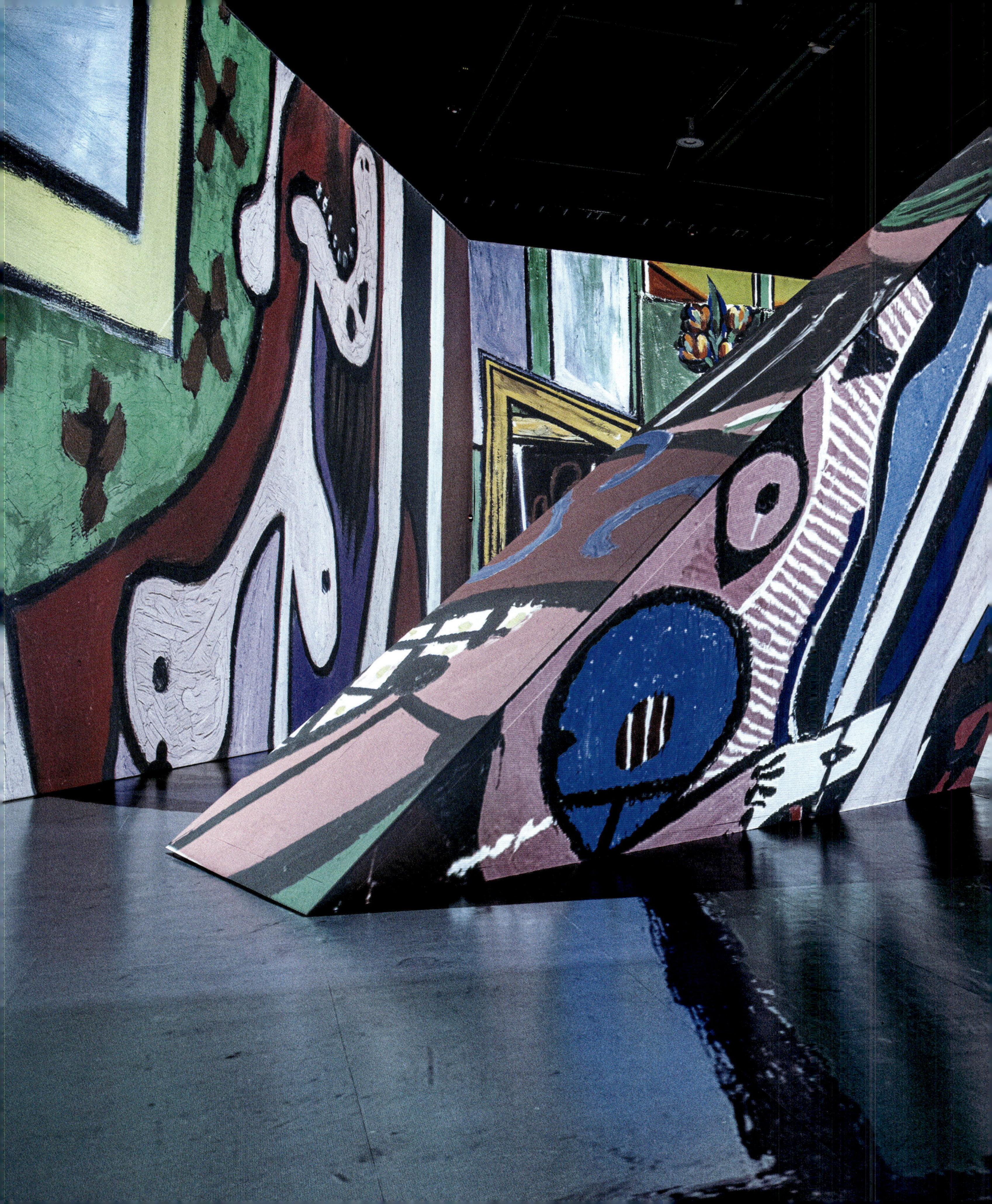

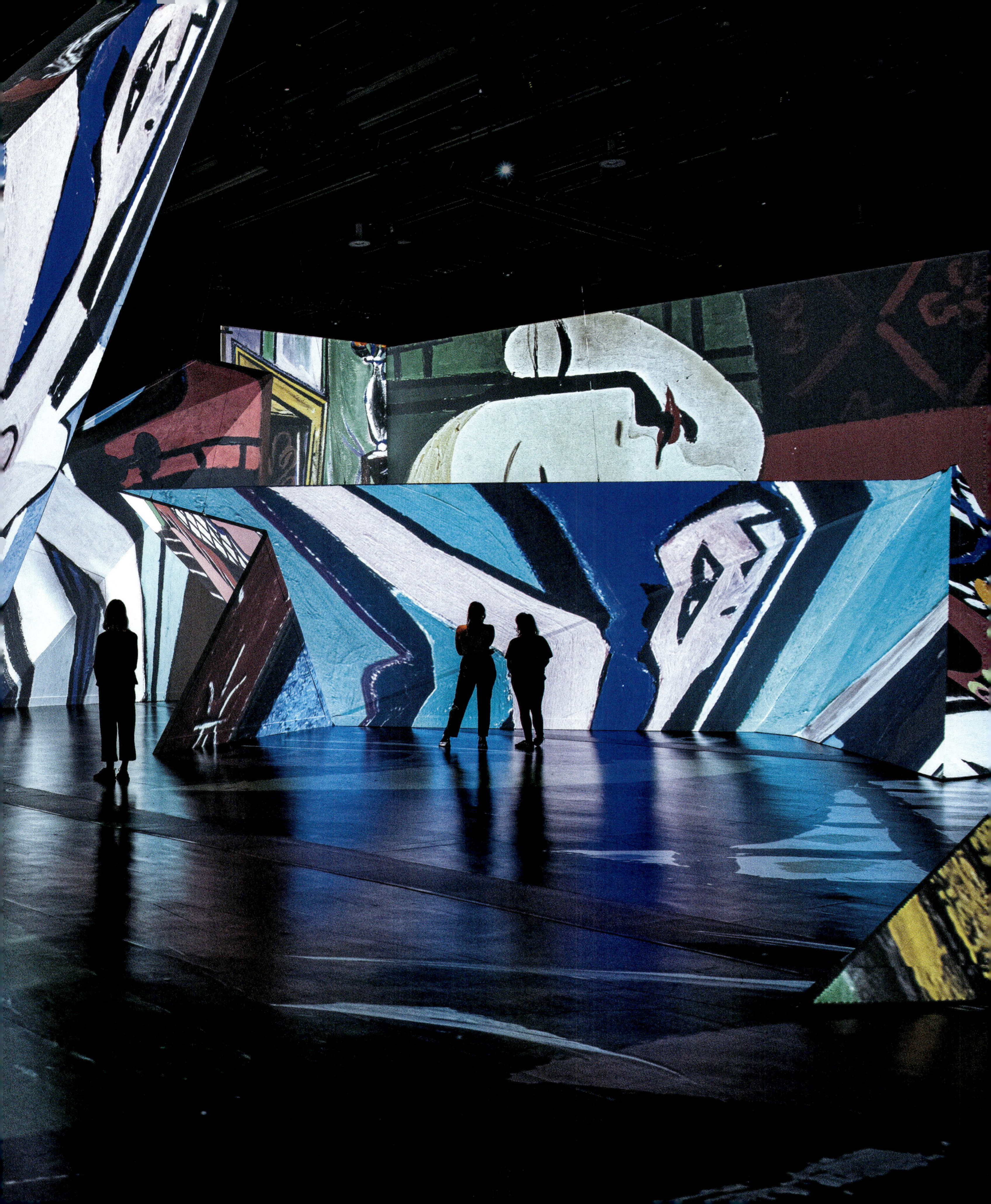

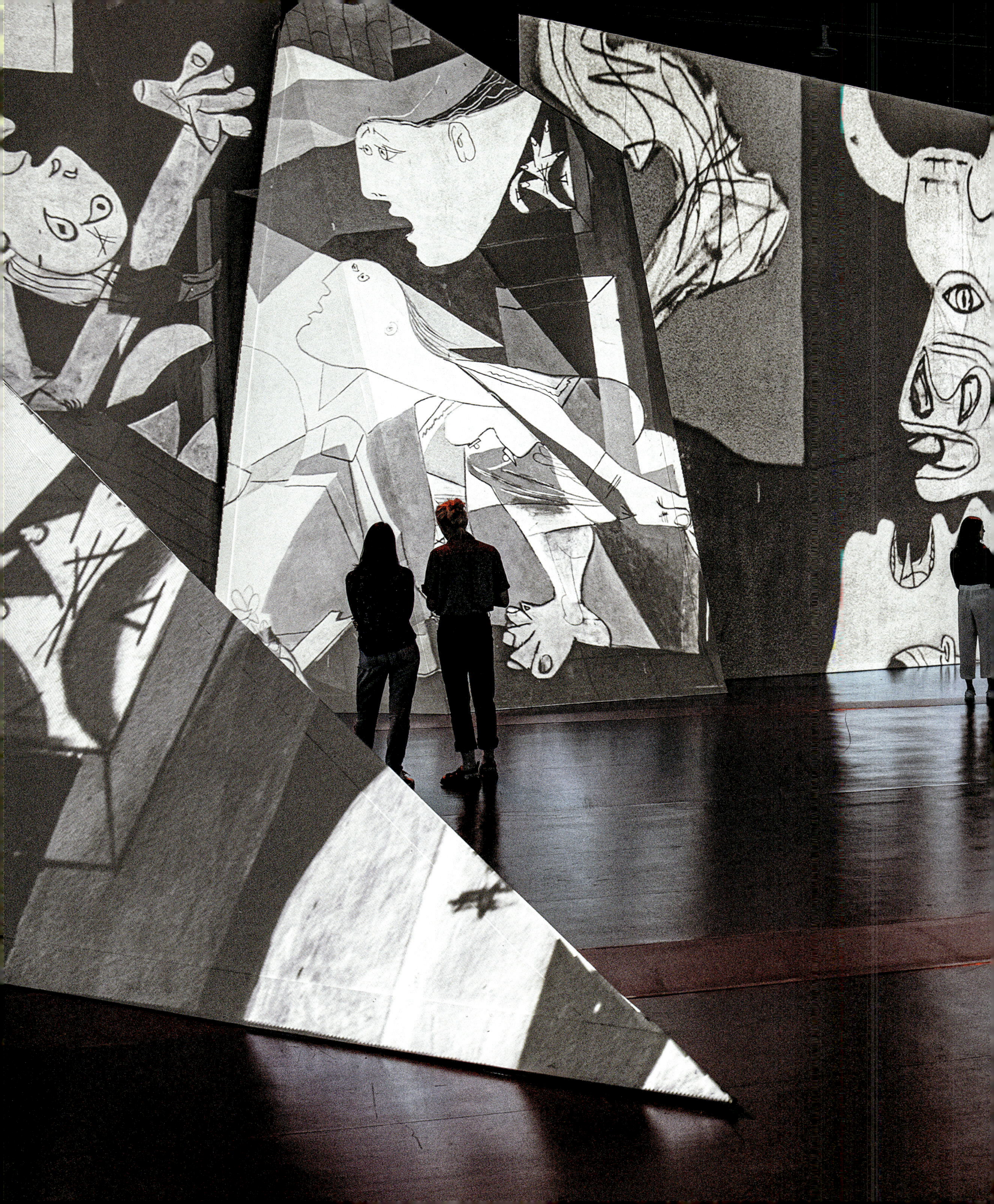

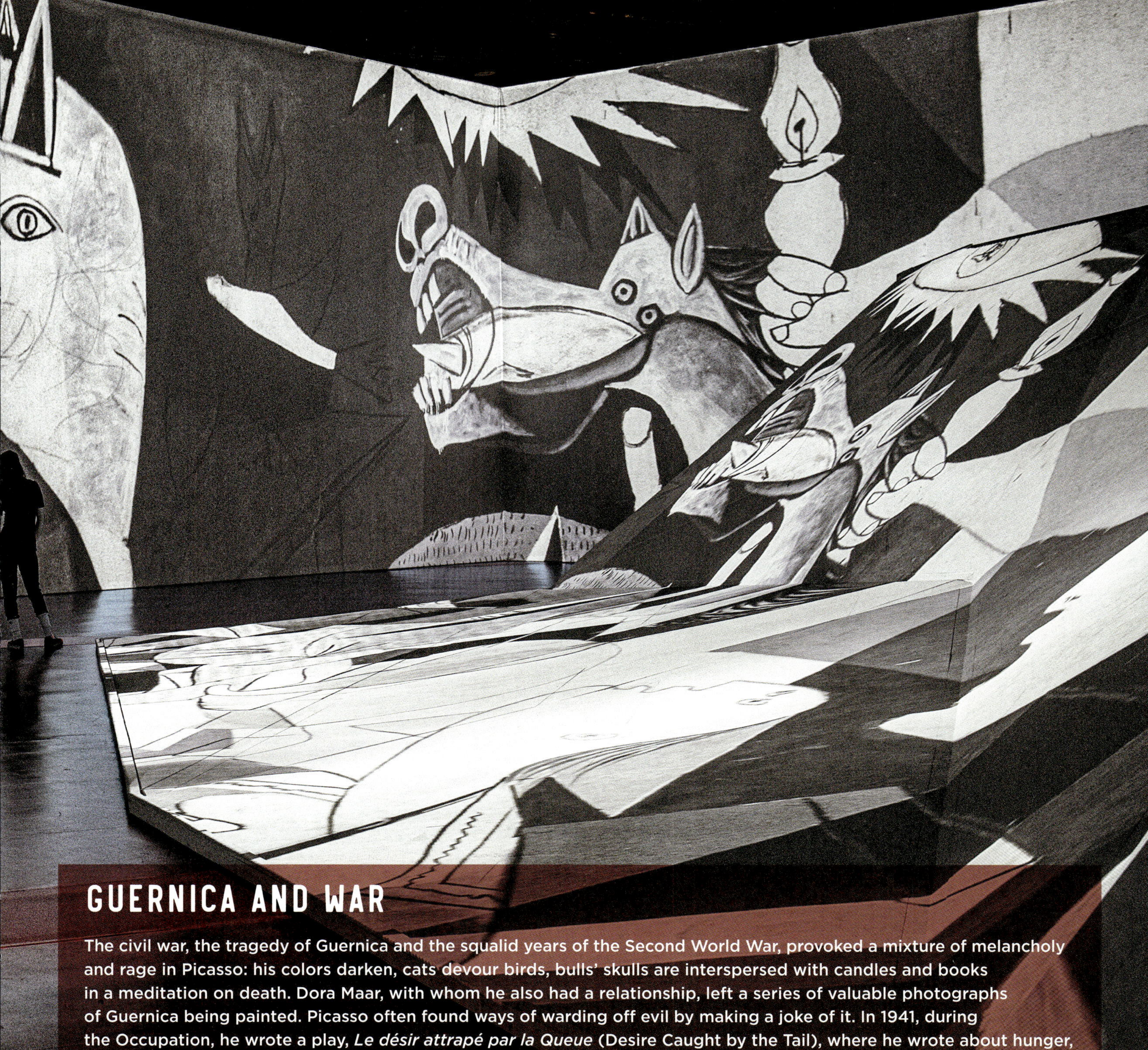

GUERNICA AND WAR

The civil war, the tragedy of Guernica and the squalid years of the Second World War, provoked a mixture of melancholy and rage in Picasso: his colors darken, cats devour birds, bulls' skulls are interspersed with candles and books in a meditation on death. Dora Maar, with whom he also had a relationship, left a series of valuable photographs of Guernica being painted. Picasso often found ways of warding off evil by making a joke of it. In 1941, during the Occupation, he wrote a play, *Le désir attrapé par la Queue* (Desire Caught by the Tail), where he wrote about hunger, cold, love and life. The reading of this play at the home of his friends Zette and Michel Leiris, in 1944, brought together actors and writers including Albert Camus, Jean-Paul Sartre, Simone de Beauvoir, Raymond Queneau and Dora Maar…

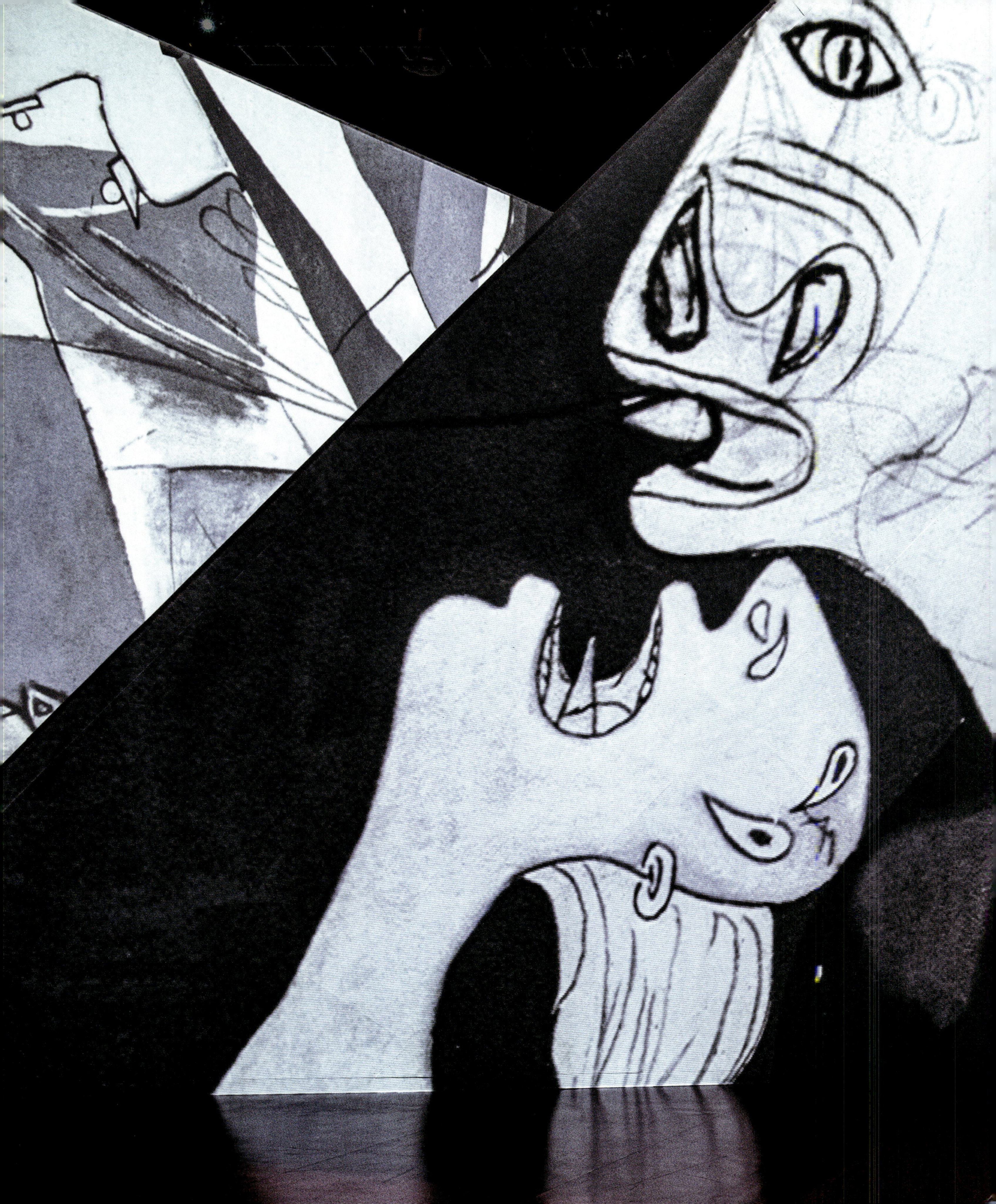

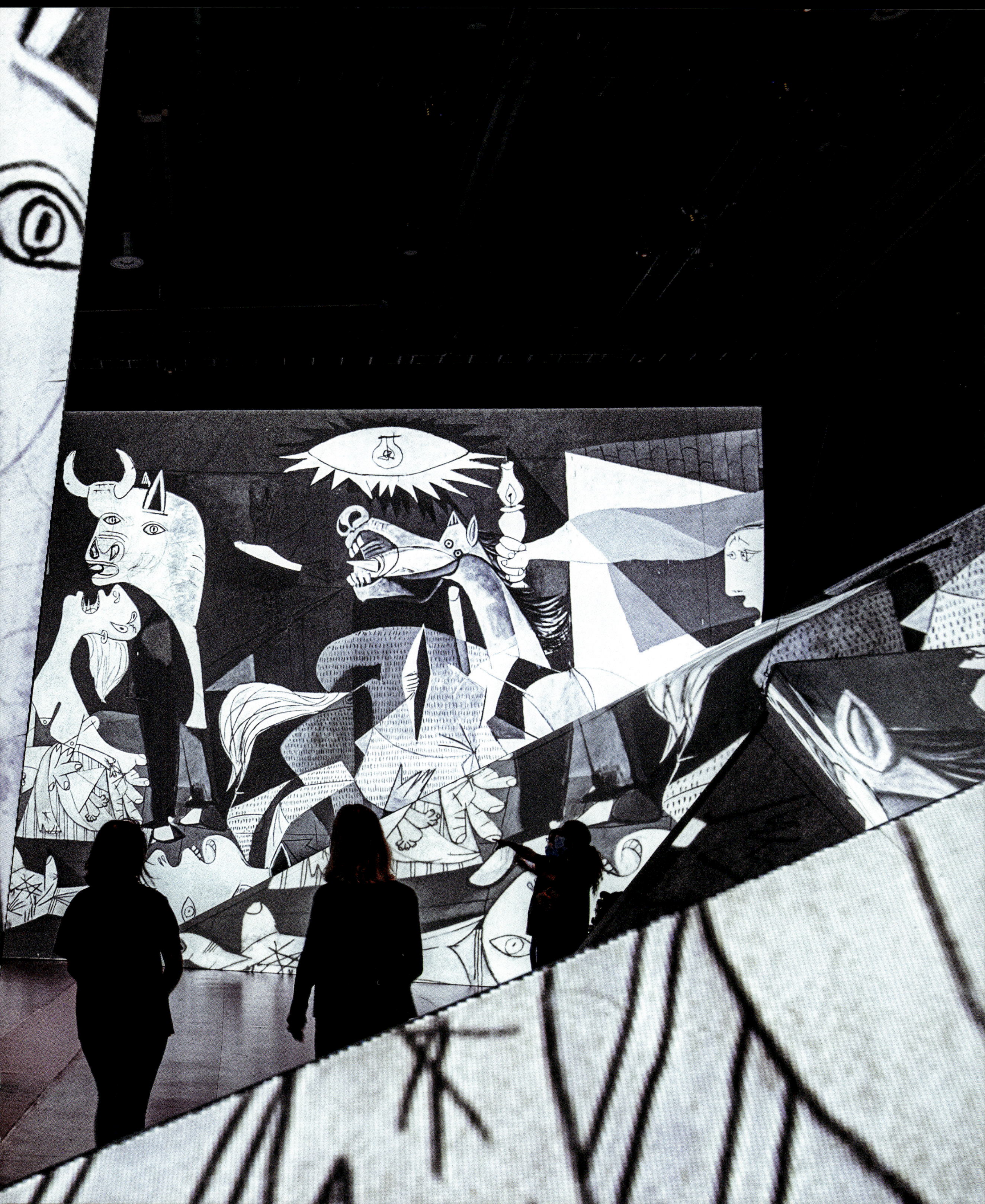

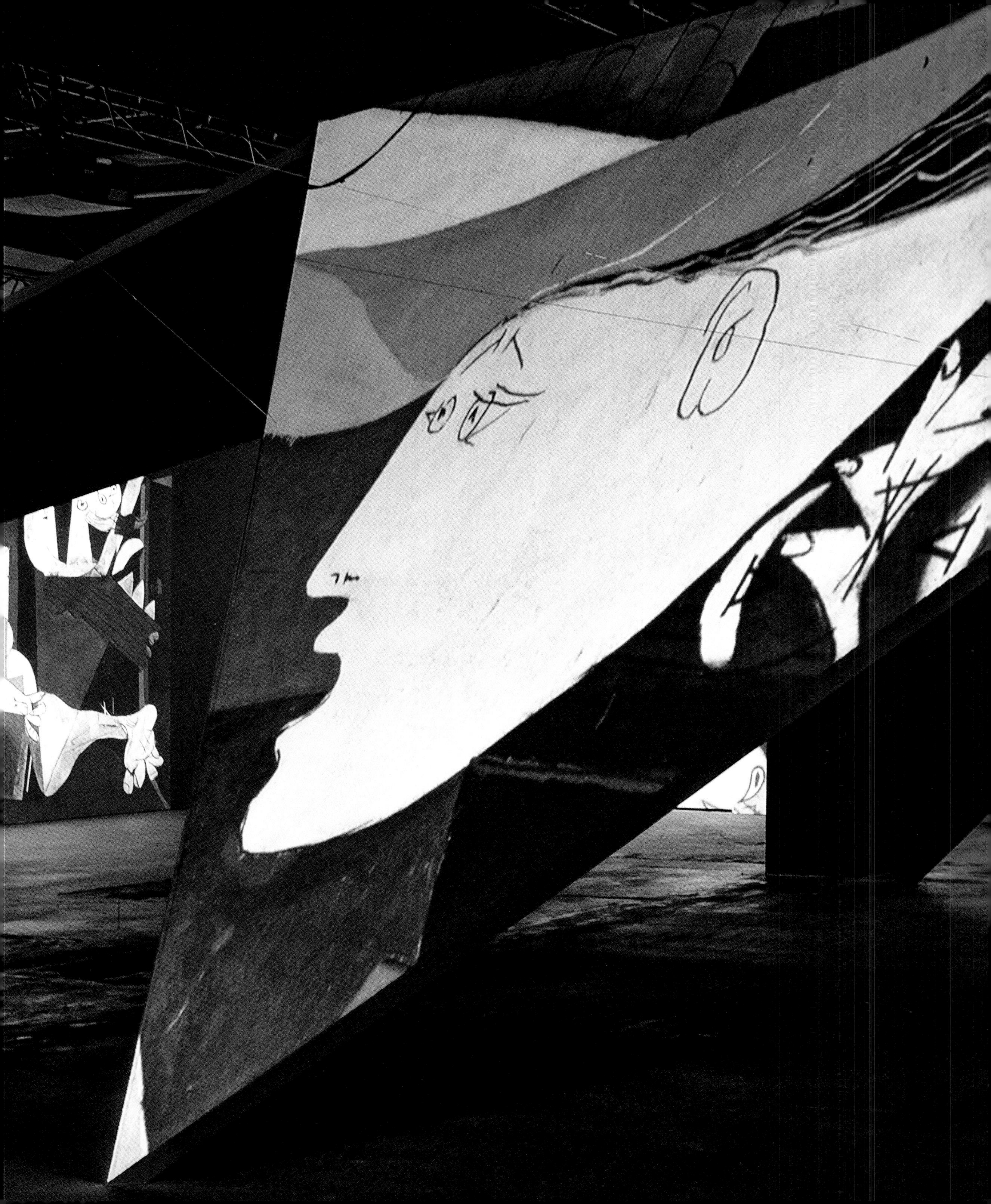

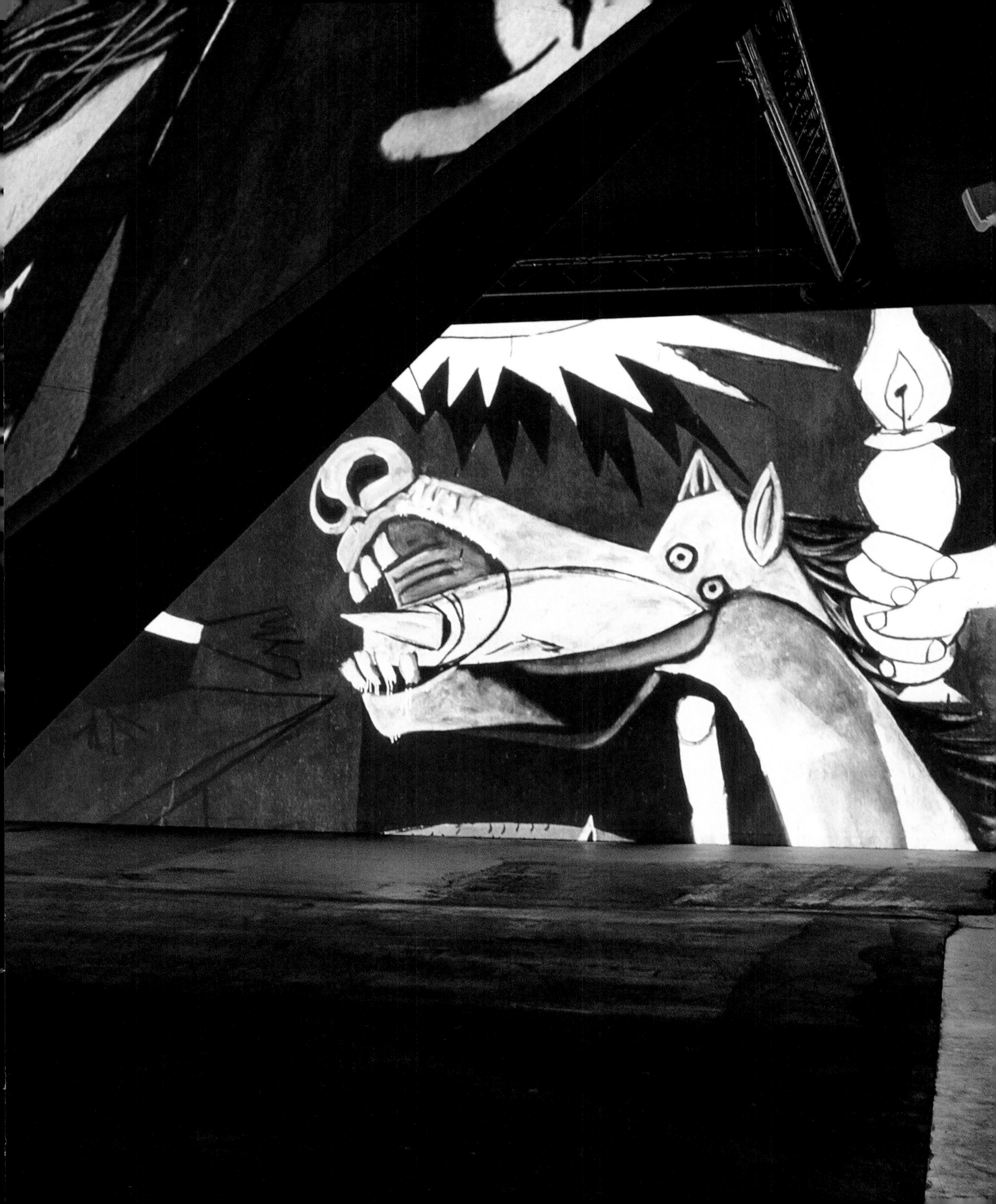

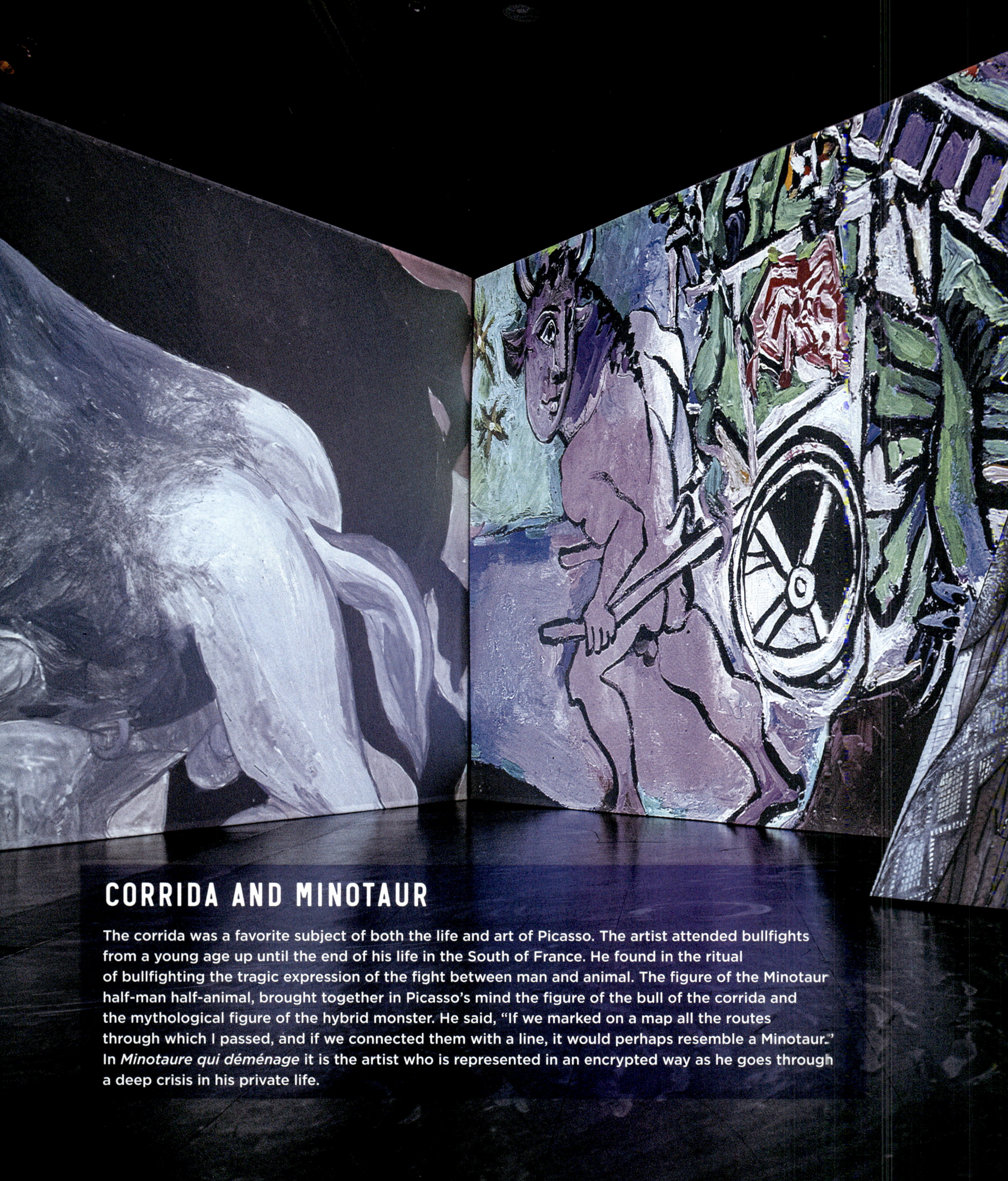

CORRIDA AND MINOTAUR

The corrida was a favorite subject of both the life and art of Picasso. The artist attended bullfights from a young age up until the end of his life in the South of France. He found in the ritual of bullfighting the tragic expression of the fight between man and animal. The figure of the Minotaur half-man half-animal, brought together in Picasso's mind the figure of the bull of the corrida and the mythological figure of the hybrid monster. He said, "If we marked on a map all the routes through which I passed, and if we connected them with a line, it would perhaps resemble a Minotaur." In *Minotaure qui déménage* it is the artist who is represented in an encrypted way as he goes through a deep crisis in his private life.

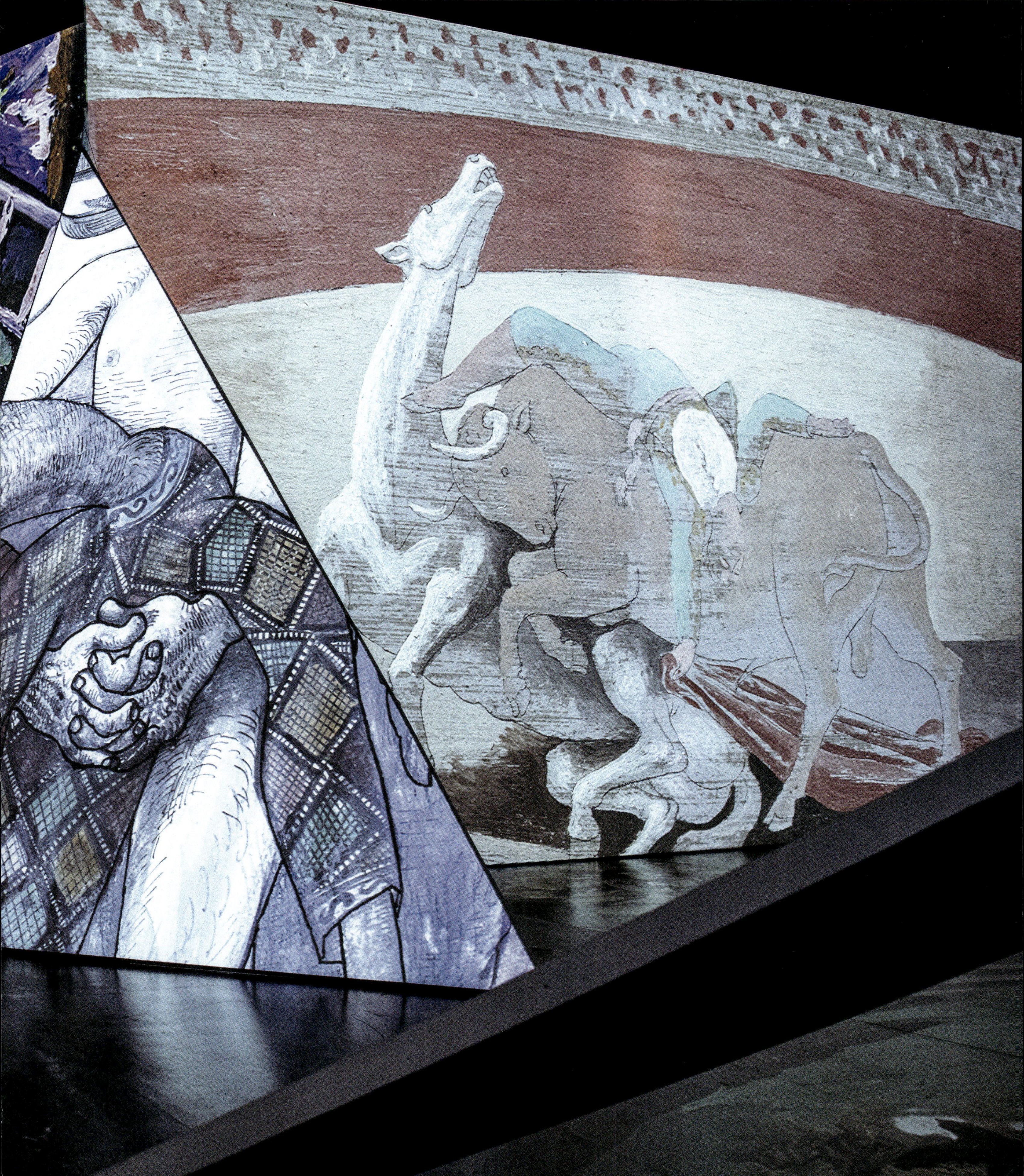

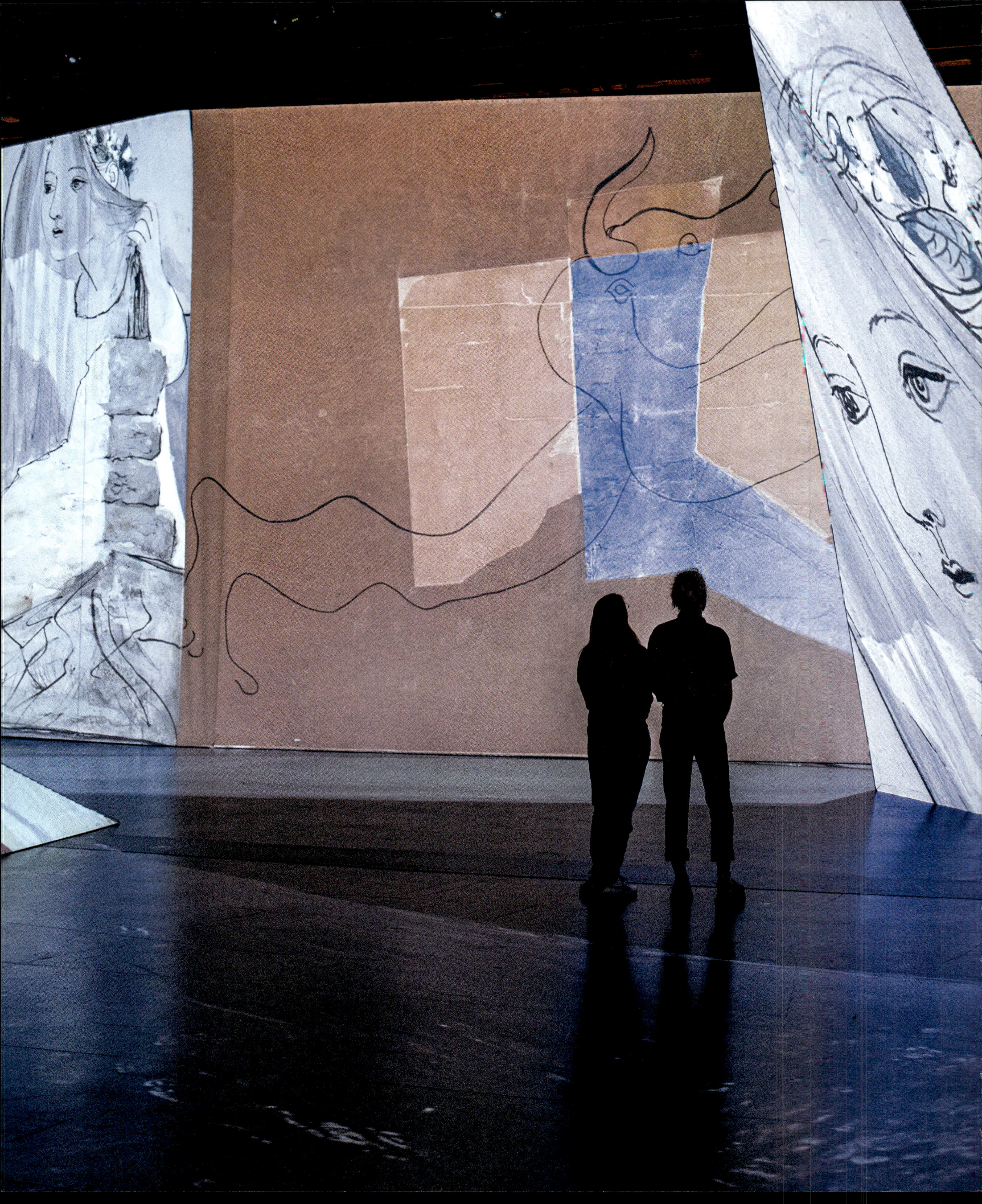

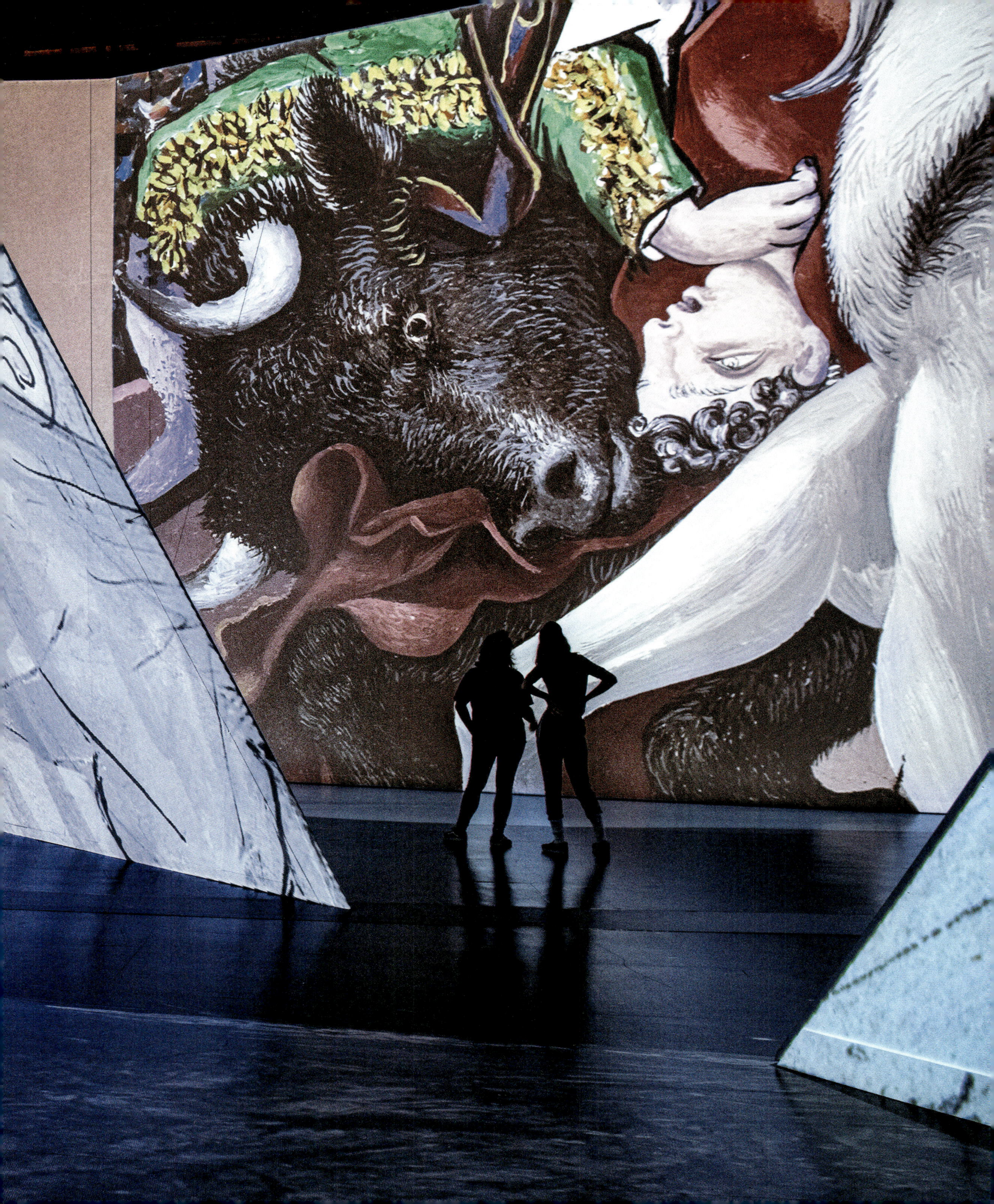

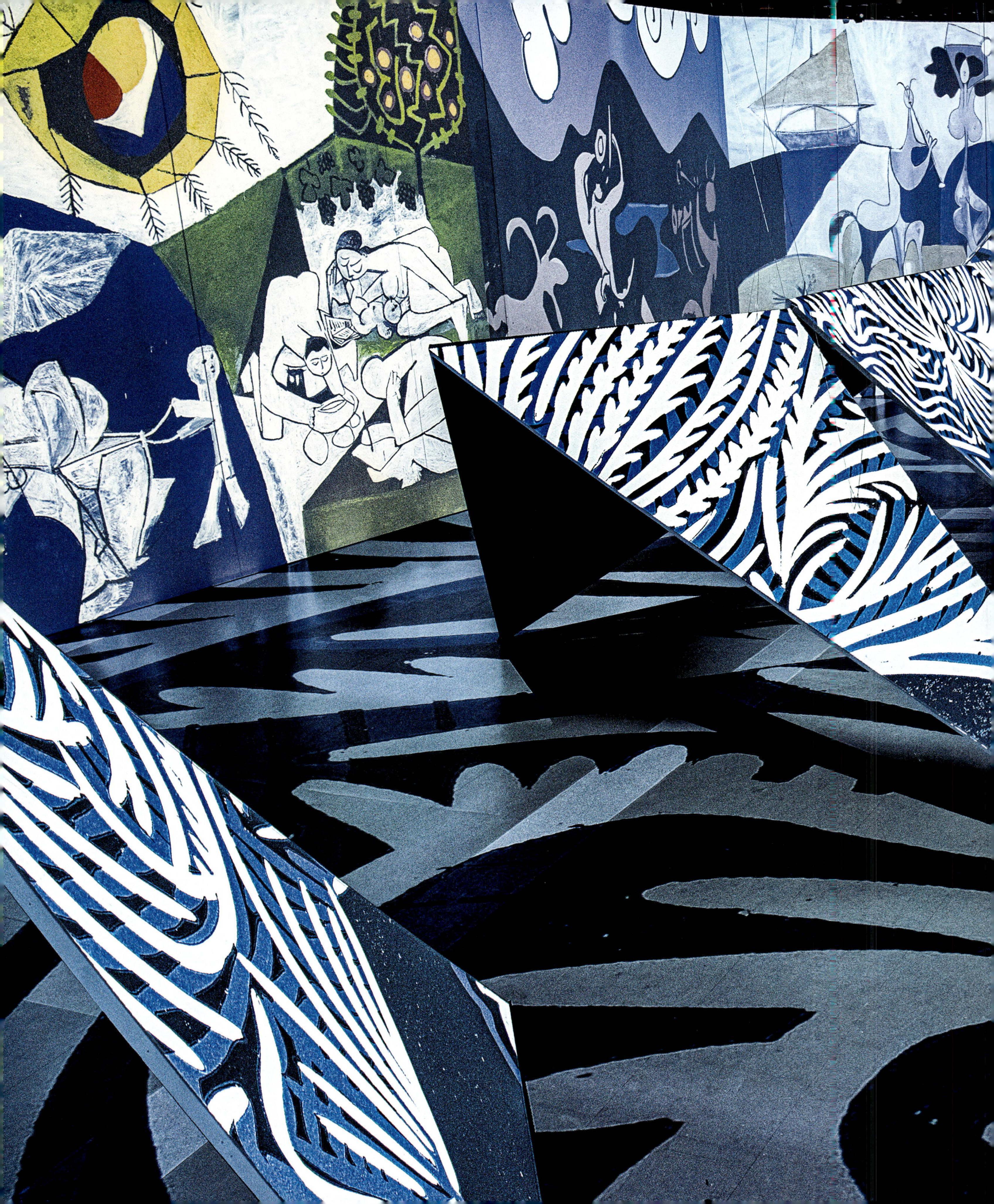

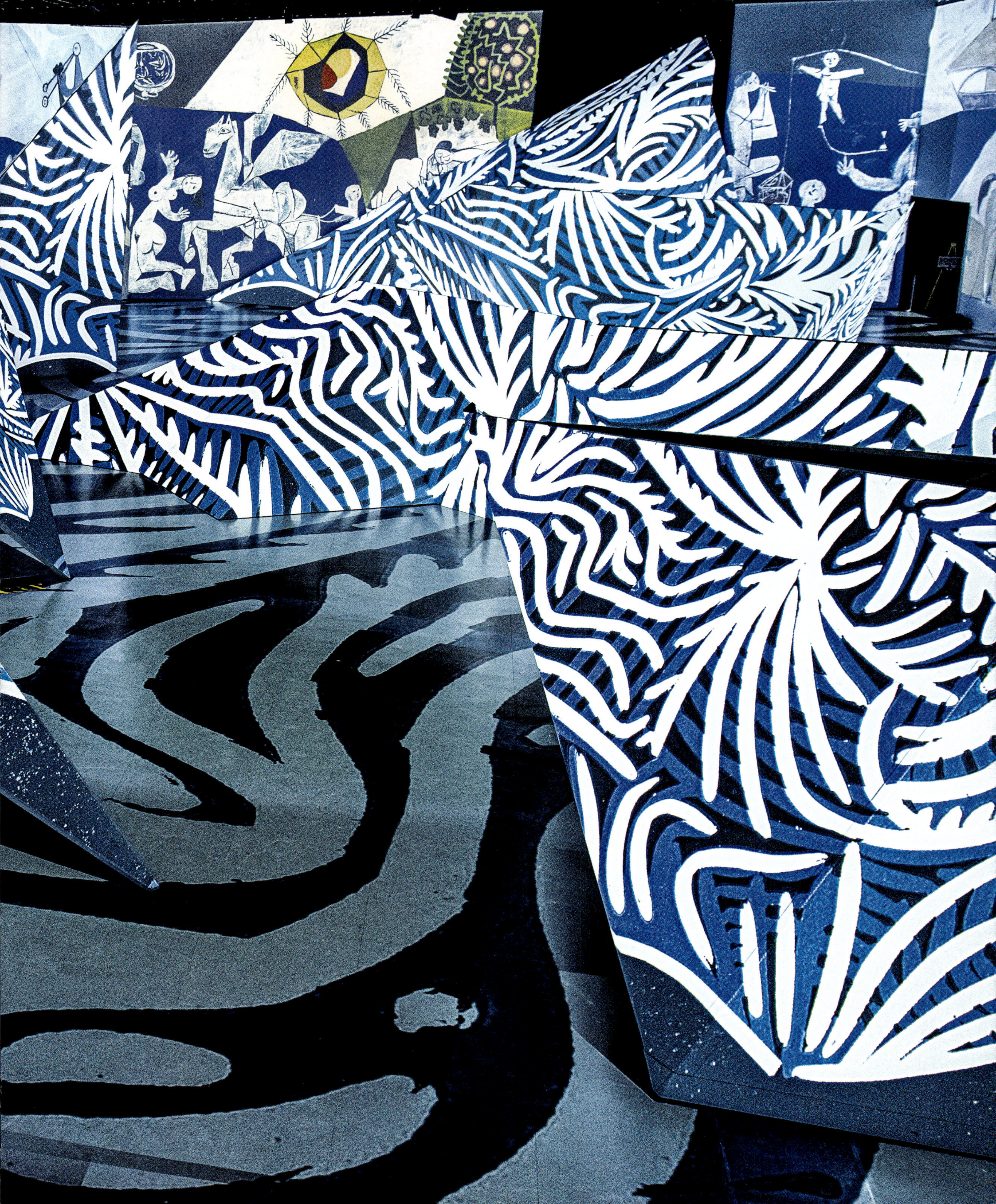

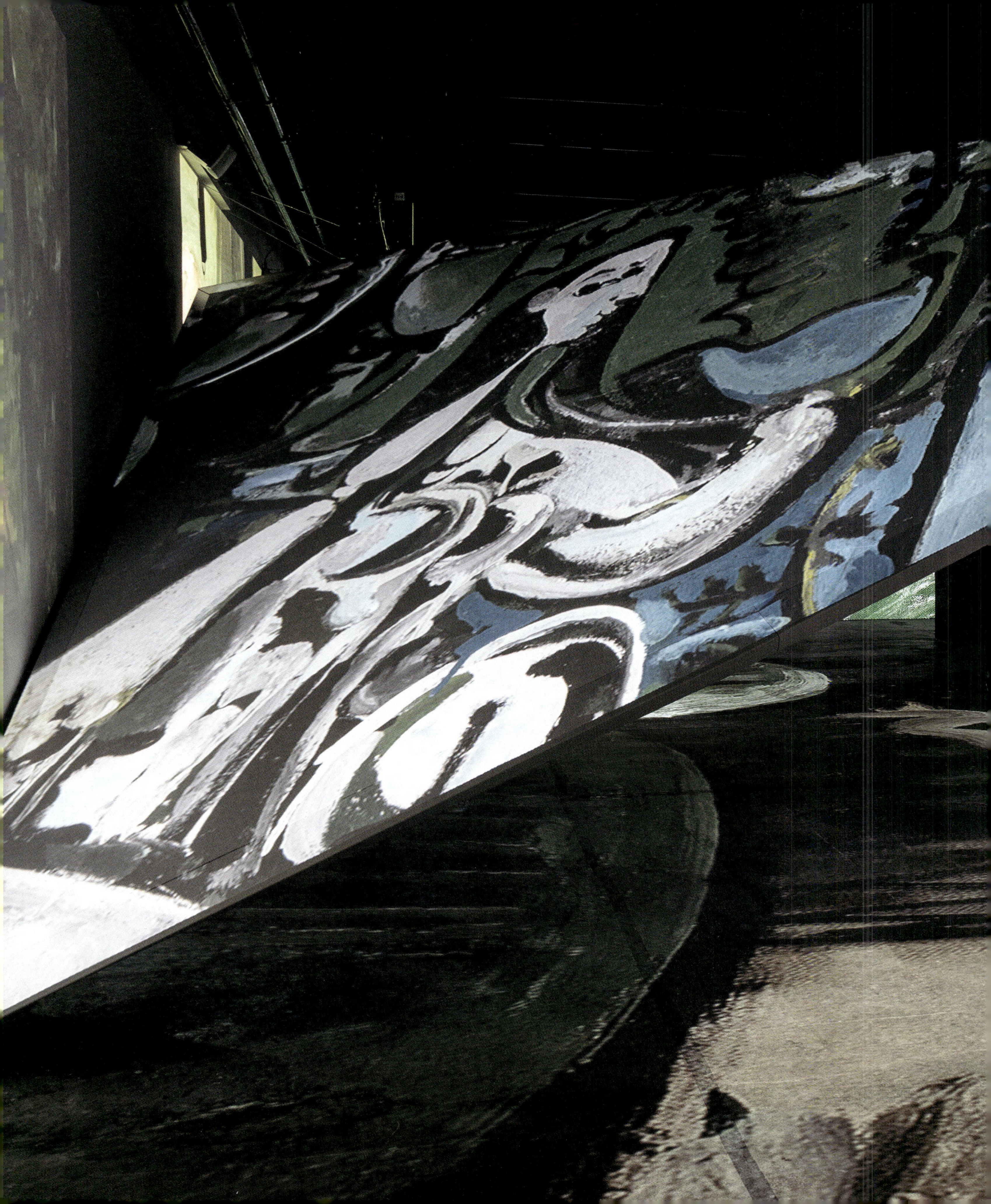

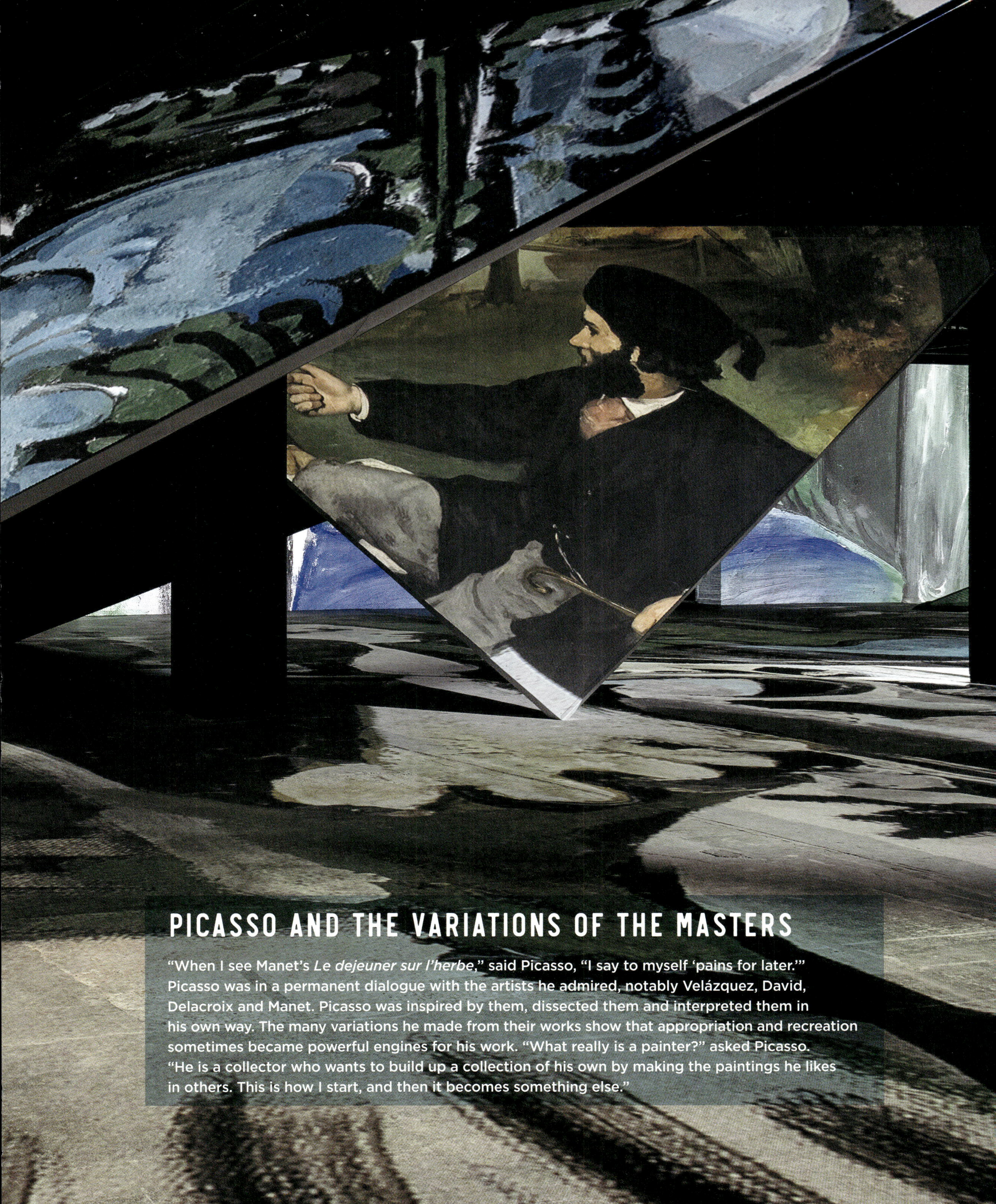

PICASSO AND THE VARIATIONS OF THE MASTERS

"When I see Manet's *Le dejeuner sur l'herbe*," said Picasso, "I say to myself 'pains for later.'"
Picasso was in a permanent dialogue with the artists he admired, notably Velázquez, David,
Delacroix and Manet. Picasso was inspired by them, dissected them and interpreted them in
his own way. The many variations he made from their works show that appropriation and recreation
sometimes became powerful engines for his work. "What really is a painter?" asked Picasso.
"He is a collector who wants to build up a collection of his own by making the paintings he likes
in others. This is how I start, and then it becomes something else."

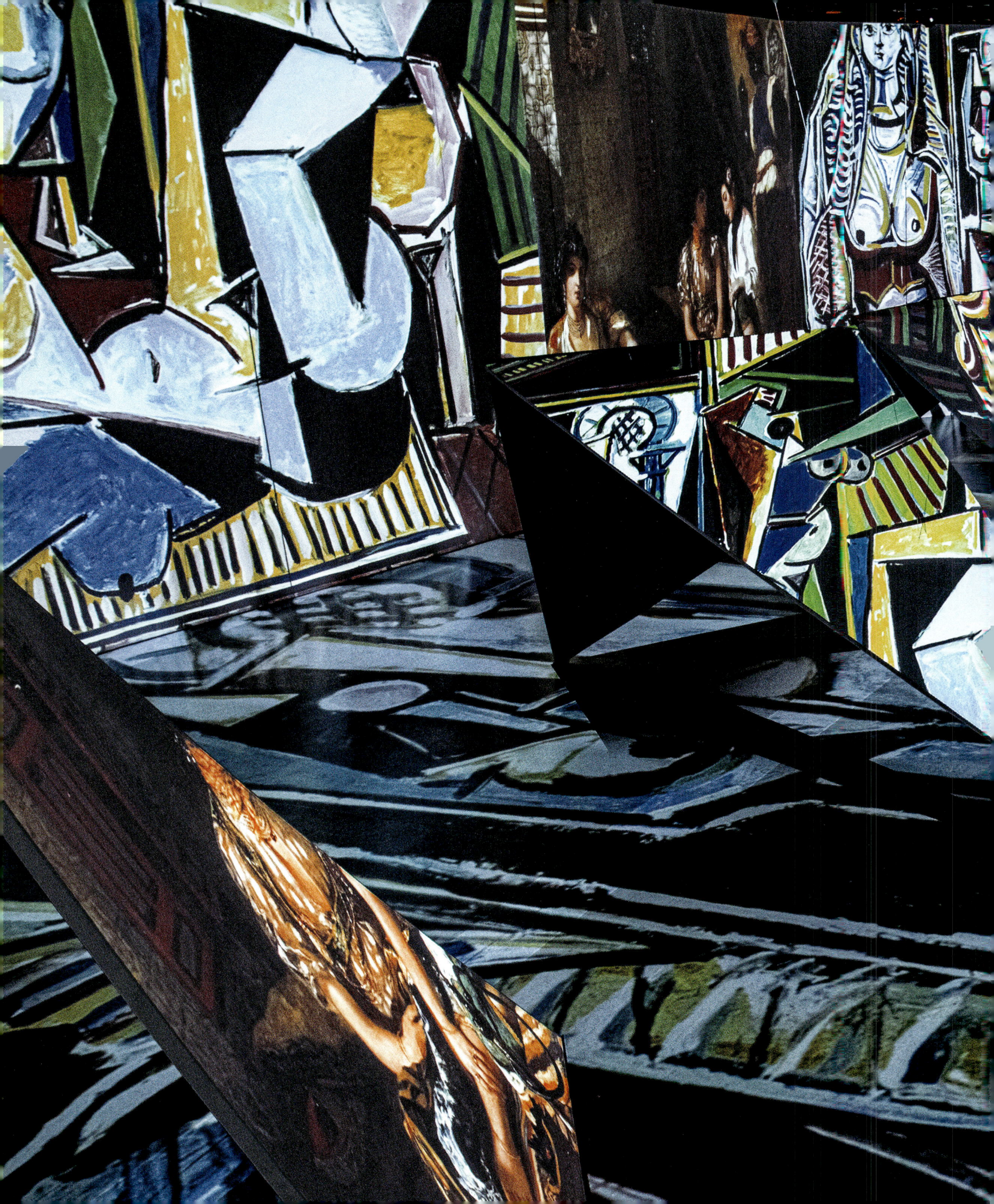

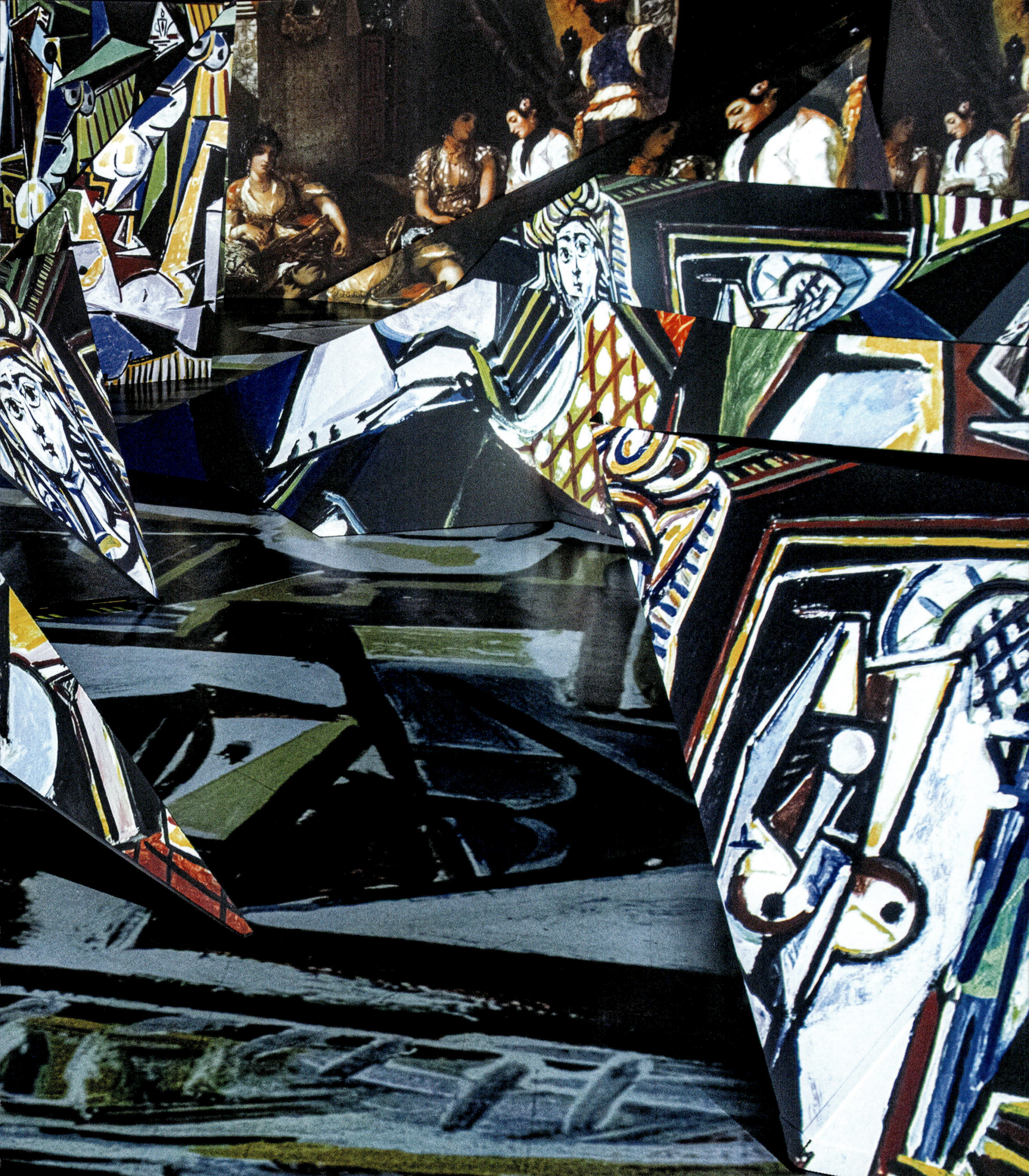

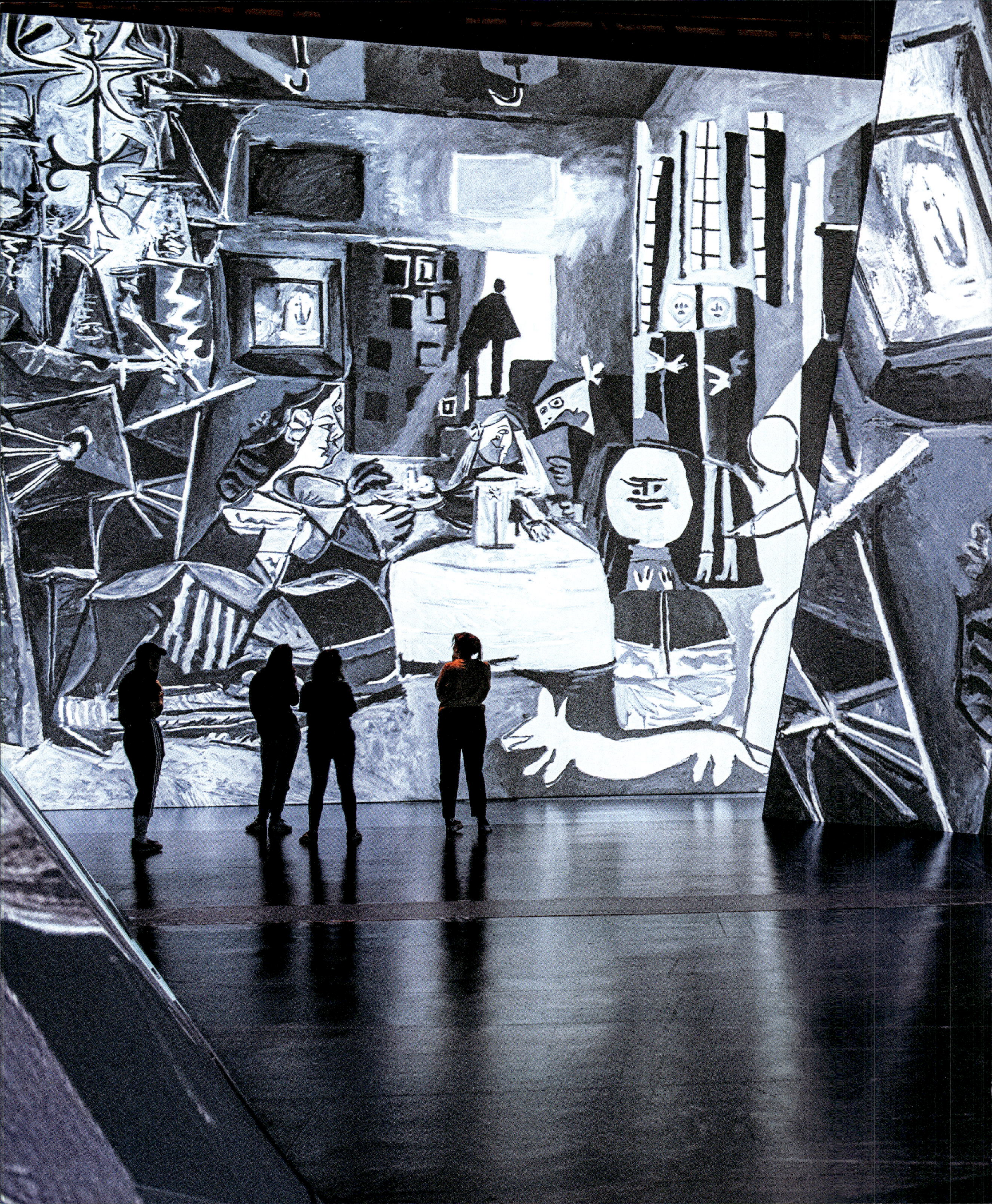

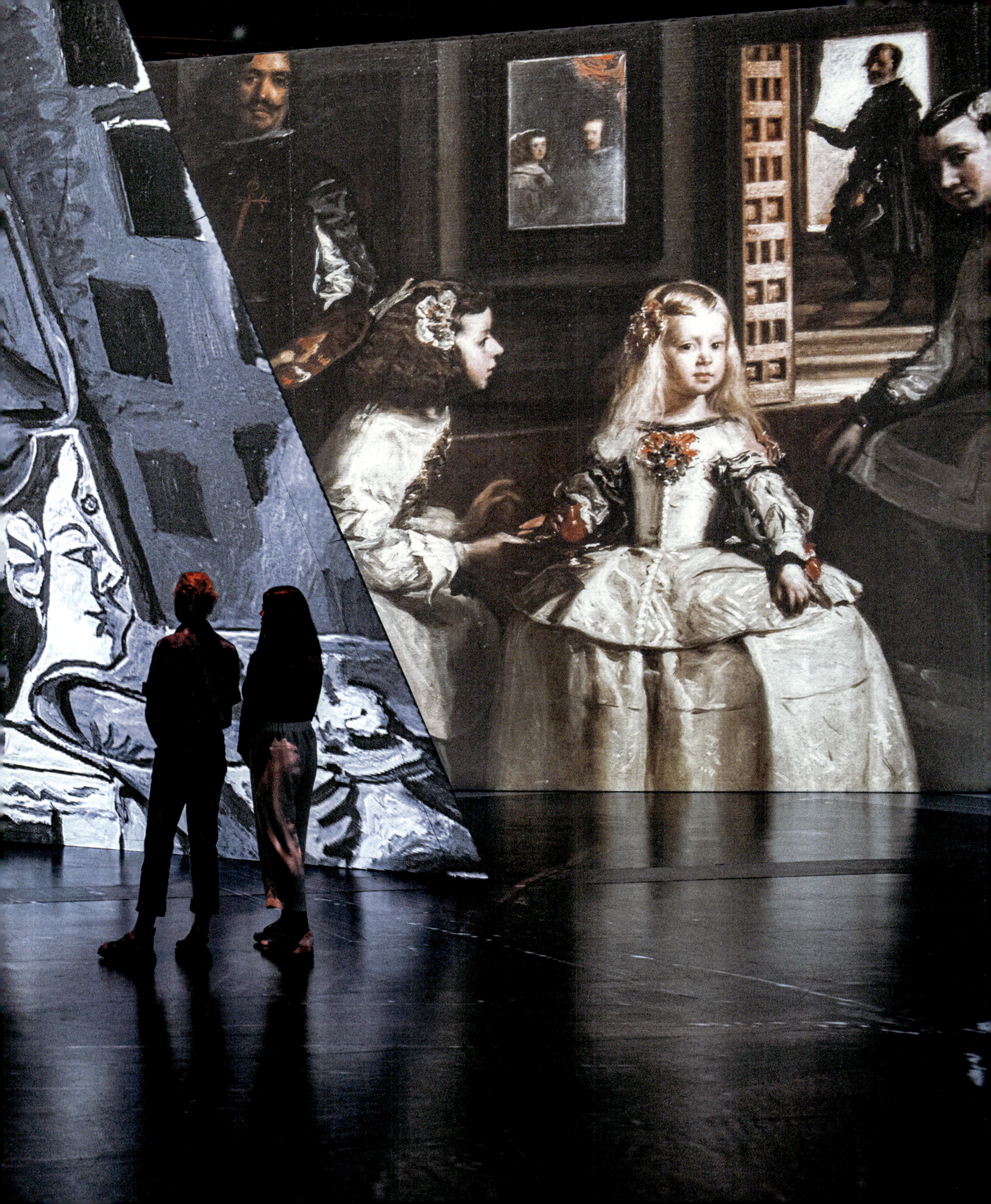

THE FINAL YEARS

In the last years of his life, Picasso was seized with a sense of urgency. He knew that he had less and less time and yet more and more things to say.
Prolific in paintings, ceramics and engravings, his last works are inhabited with musketeers, matadors, maternities and embraces, as many subjects that touched the deepest part of his manhood: literary references, memories of Spain, eroticism, self-portraits which are imbued with the tragic sense of death.

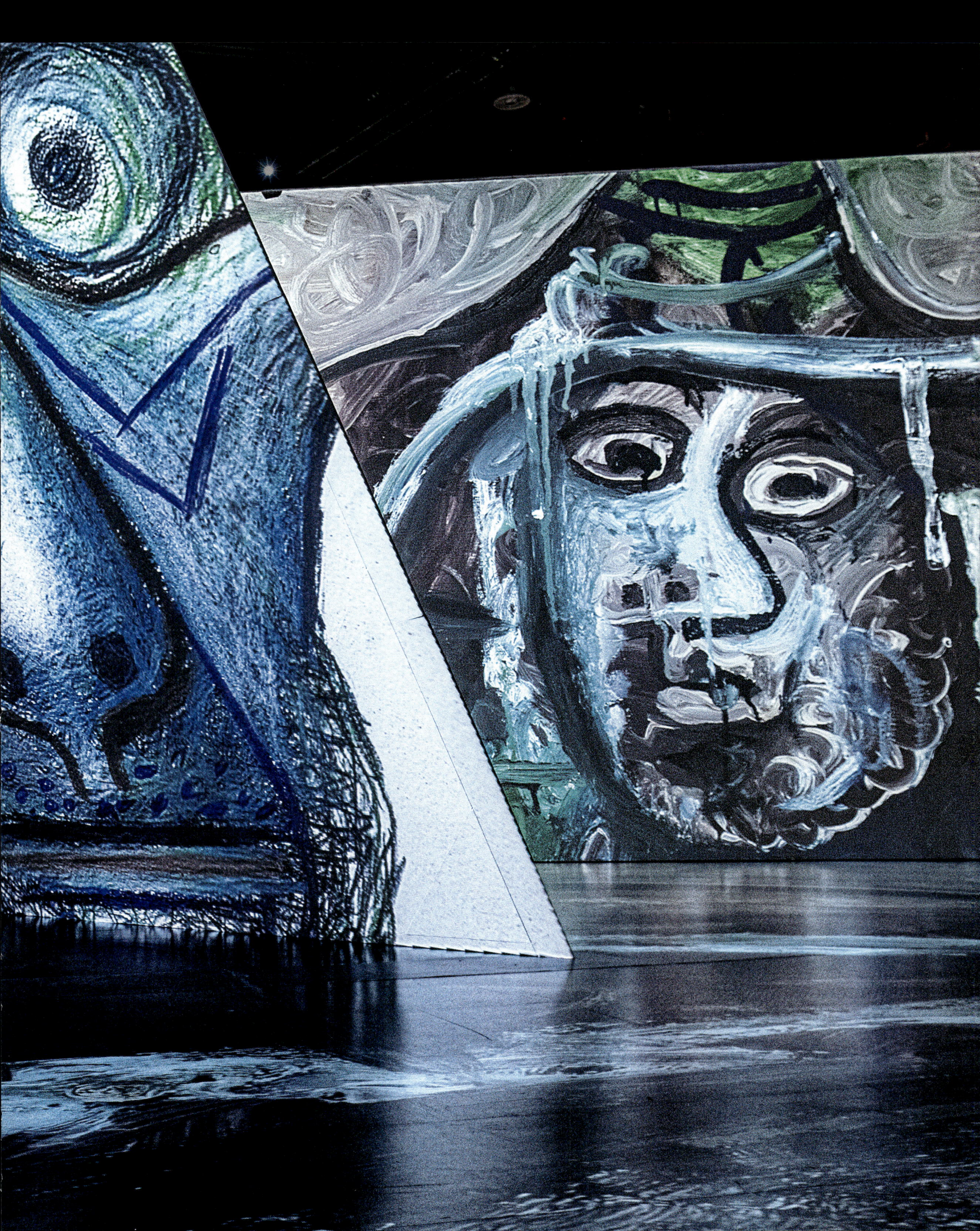

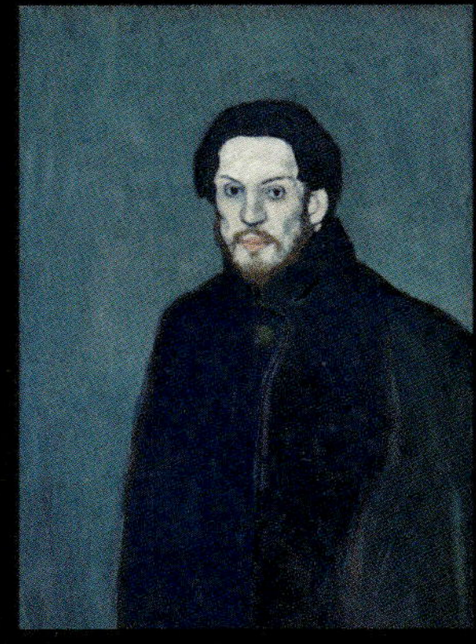

Autoportrait, 1901
Oil on canvas
81 × 60 cm - 31 ⁷/₈ × 23 ⁵/₈ in
Musée national Picasso, Paris

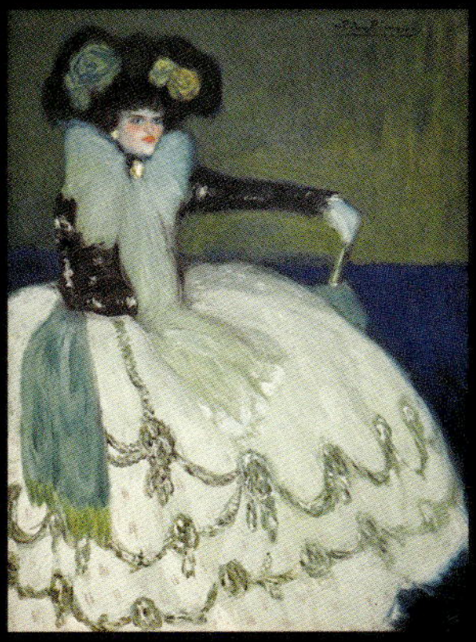

La femme en bleu, 1901
Oil on canvas
133 × 100 cm - 52 ³/₈ × 39 ³/₈ in
Museo nacional centro de Arte Reina Sofia, Madrid

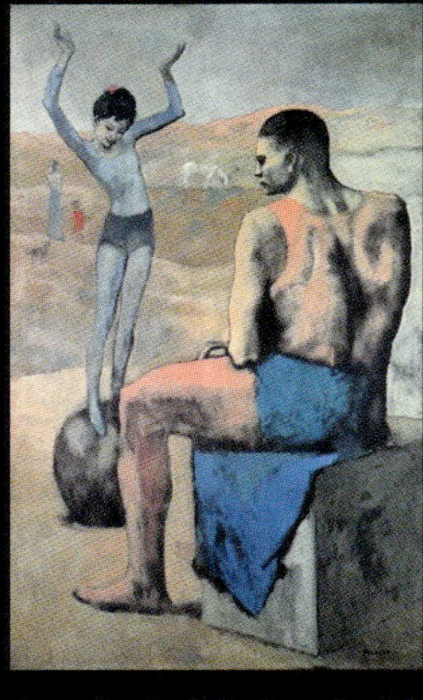

Acrobate à la boule, 1905
Oil on canvas
147 × 95 cm - 57 ⁷/₈ × 37 ½ in
The Pushkin State Museum of Fine Arts, Moscow

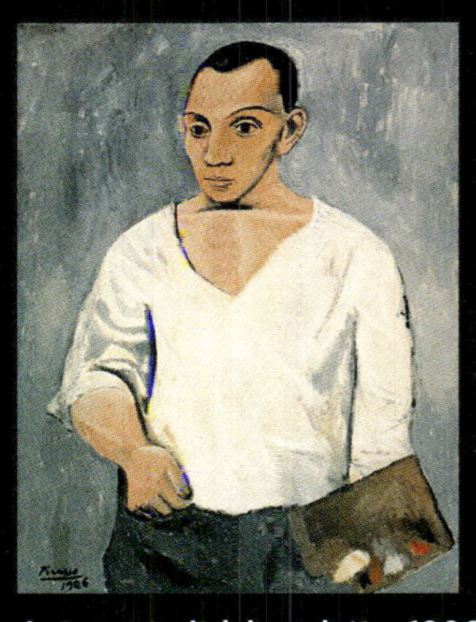

Autoportrait à la palette, 1906
Oil on canvas
91.9 × 73.3 cm - 36 ³/₁₆ × 28 ⁷/₈ in
The Philadelphia Museum of Art, Philadelphia

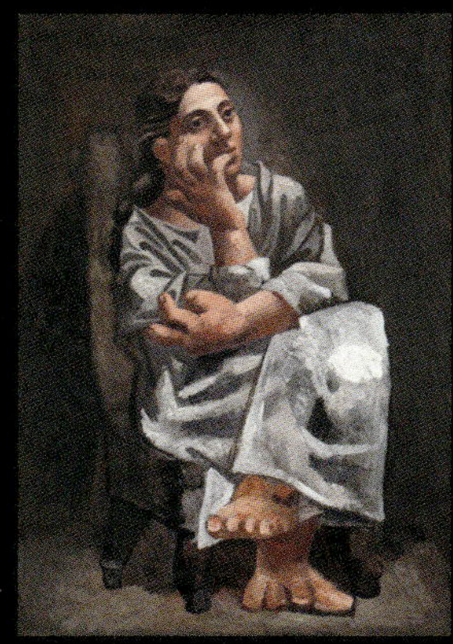

Femme assise, 1920
Oil on canvas
92 × 65 cm - 36 ¼ × 25 ⁹/₁₆ in
Musée national Picasso, Paris

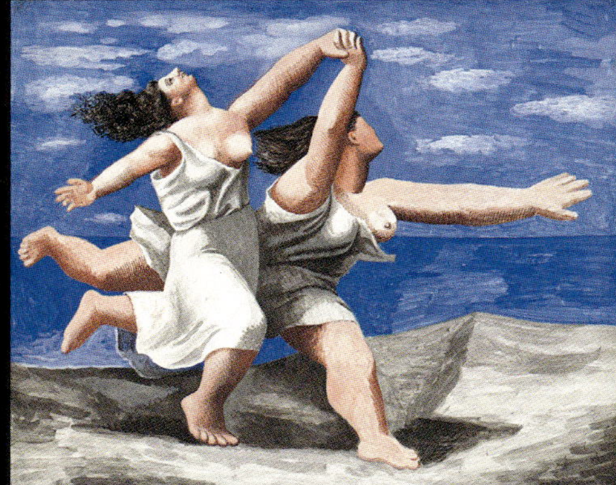

Deux femmes courant sur la plage, 1922
Gouache on plywood
32.5 × 41.1 cm - 12 ¾ × 16 ¹/₈ in
Musée national Picasso, Paris

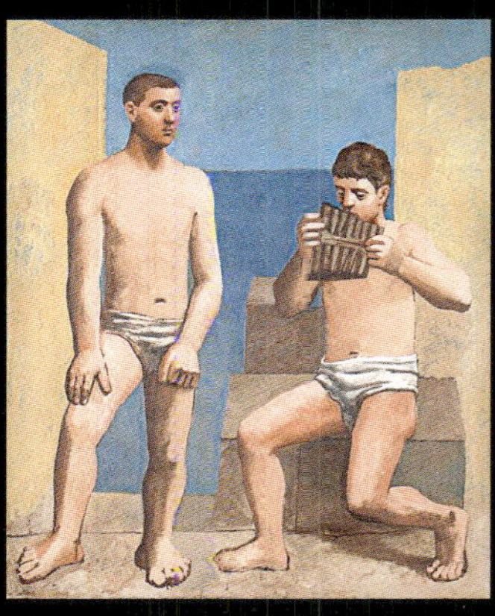

La flûte de Pan, 1923
Oil on canvas
205 × 174 cm - 80 ¹¹/₁₆ × 68 ½ in
Musée national Picasso, Paris

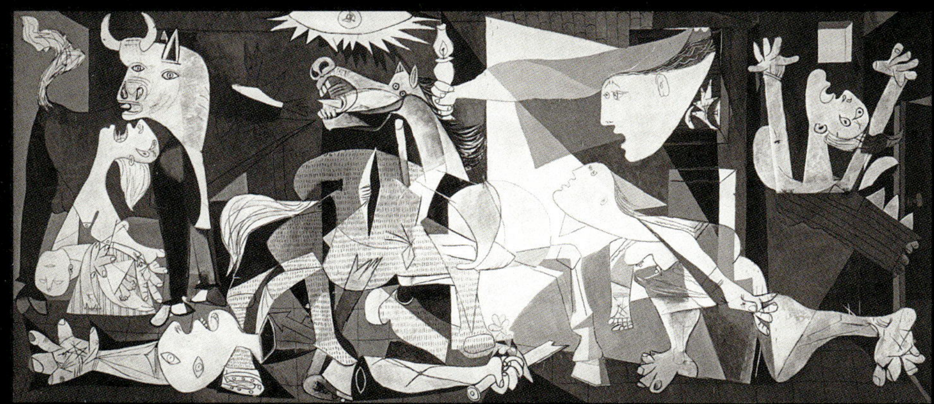

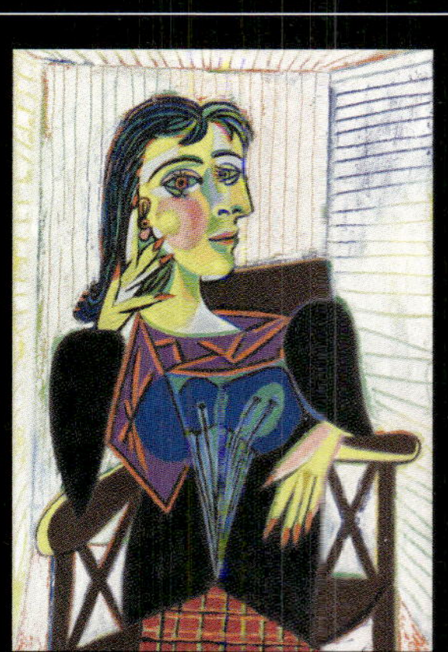

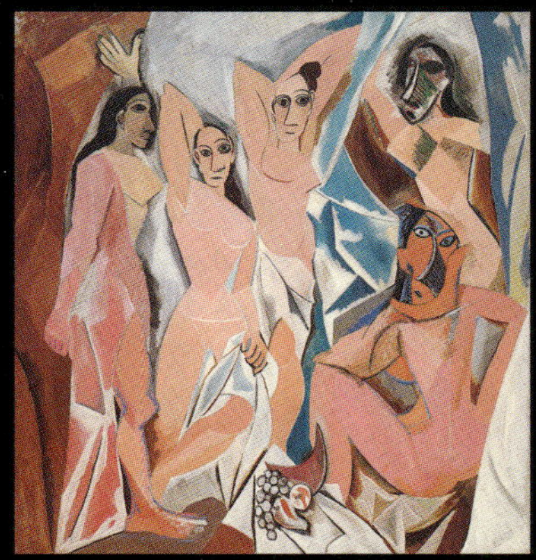

Les demoiselles d'Avignon, 1907
Oil on canvas
243.9 × 233.7 cm - 96 × 92 in
Museum of Modern Art, New York

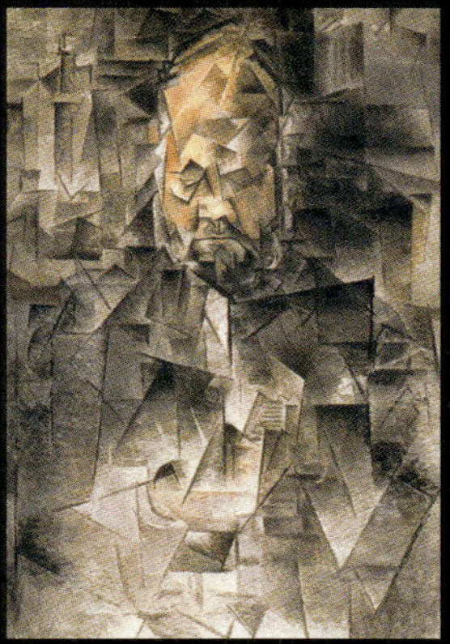

Portrait d'Antoine Vollard, 1910
Oil on canvas
92 × 65 cm - 36 ¼ × 25 ⁹/₈ in
The Pushkin State Museum of Fine Arts, Moscow

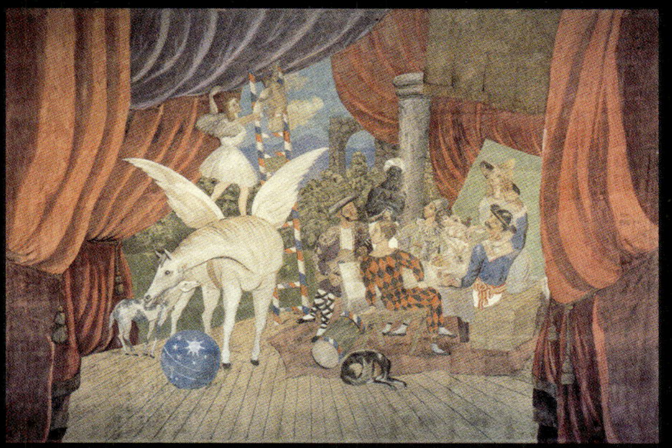

Rideau de scène du ballet "Parade", 1917
Glue-based paint on canvas
1050 × 1640 cm - 413 ³/₈ × 645 ¹¹/₁₆ in
Centre Pompidou - Musée national d'art moderne, Paris

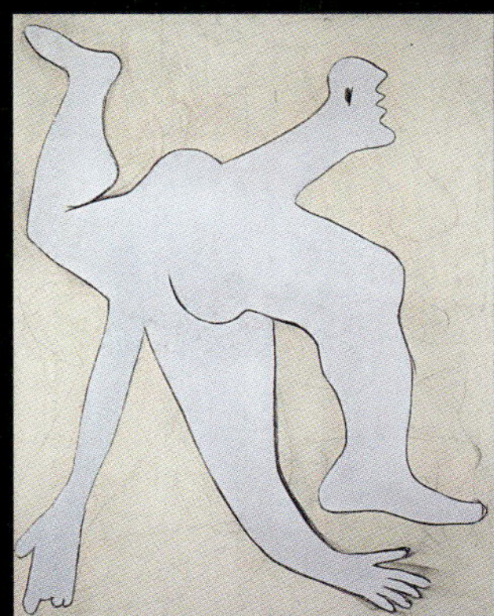

Acrobate bleu, 1929
Charcoal and oil on canvas
162 × 130 cm - 63 ¾ × 51 ¹/₈ in
Musée national Picasso, Paris

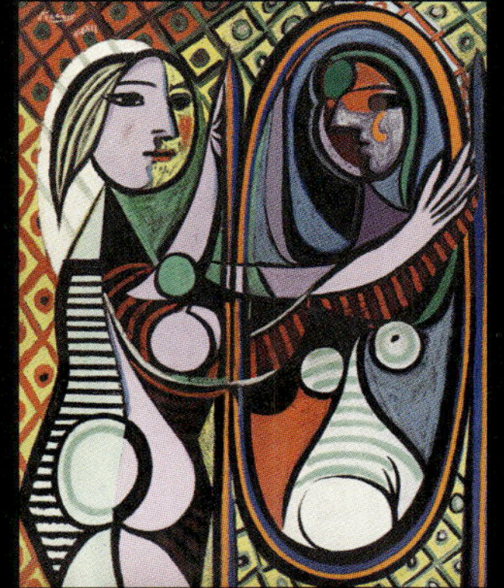

Jeune fille devant un miroir, 1932
Oil on canvas
162.3 × 130.2 cm - 64 × 51 ¼ in
Museum of Modern Art, New York

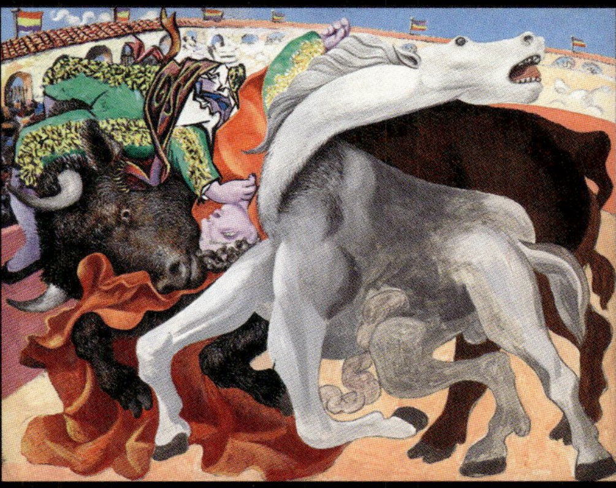

La mort du torero, 1933
Oil on wood
31 × 40 cm - 12 ³/₁₆ × 15 ¾ in
Musée national Picasso, Paris

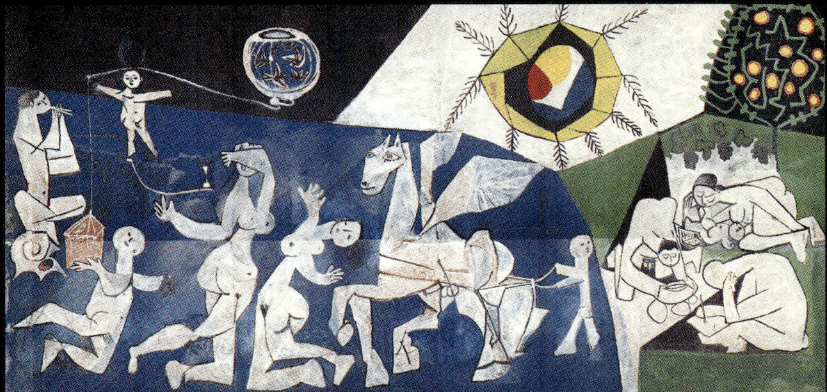

La guerre et la paix, 1952
Oil on wood
4.7 × 10.2 m - 185 ¹/₁₆ × 401 ⁹/₁₆ in
Chapelle de Vallauris, France

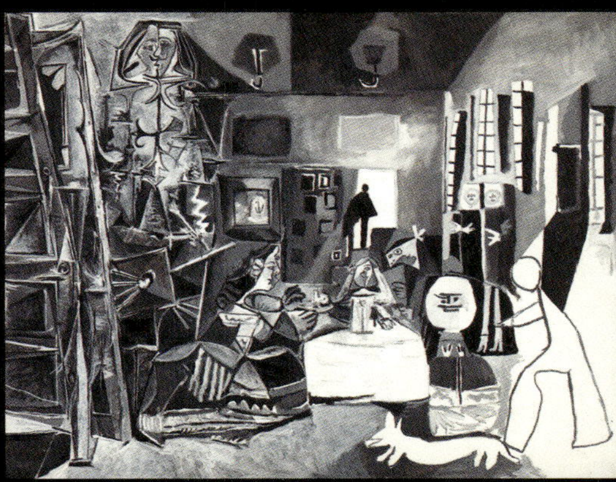

Les Ménines d'après Vélasquez, 1957
Oil on canvas
194 × 260 cm - 76 ³/₈ × 102 ³/₈ in
Musée Picasso, Barcelona

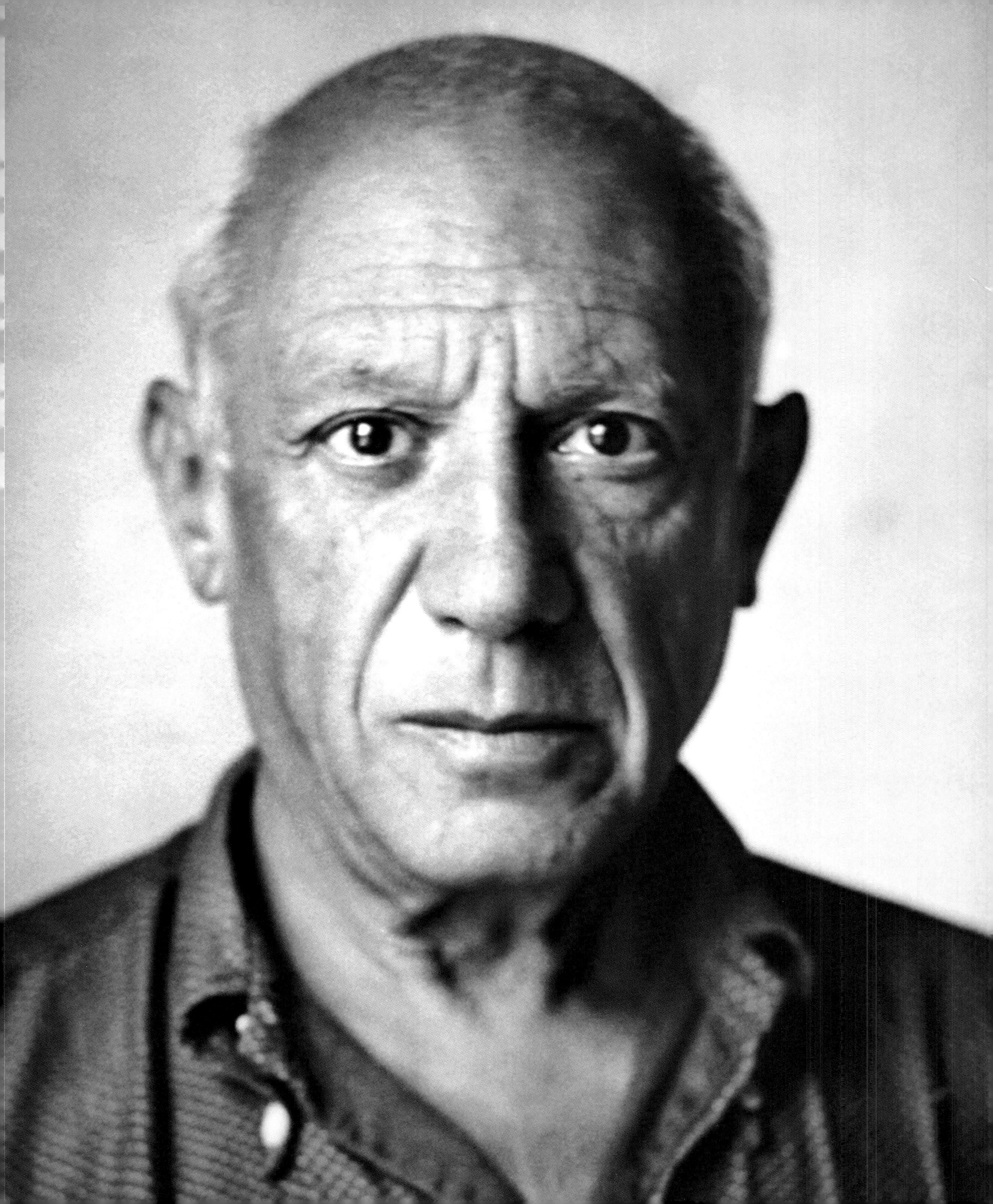

BIOGRAPHY

1881 Picasso was born in Malaga, where he lived until the age of eight. In 1889, the whole family moved to La Coruña as his father was appointed professor of drawing at the Instituto da Guarda. Picasso attended drawing classes there.

1895 The family moved to Barcelona. At the age of 15, Picasso participated in the Exhibition of Fine Arts and Industry with *First Communion*. At the famous cabaret Els 4 Gats, he became friends with many poets, artists and intellectuals.

1900 First stay in Paris where he exhibited at the Exposition Universelle. During his blue period, he plunged his gaze into human destiny, with subjects such as those on the fringes of society, single women, the elderly or the blind. In 1904, he settled permanently in the Bateau-Lavoir in Paris. This was the beginning of his pink period where the world of the circus and the landscapes of Gósol predominate.

1907 With *Les demoiselles d'Avignon*, Picasso created an entirely new modern space, announcing cubism and testifying to his interest in non-Western art, particularly African art. From 1908 to 1918, he continued to explore cubism.

1912 With *Nature morte à la chaise cannée* (1912), Picasso created the first artistic collage of the century: a piece of waxed canvas imitating chair caning and framed with a real rope. In his sculpture *Le verre d'absinthe* (1914) made in several variations, he introduced a real spoon.

1917 During his collaboration with Serge de Diaghilev for the avant-garde Ballets russes, Picasso mixed all styles without worrying about classifications. His art was used for the sets, costumes and stage curtains of the ballet *Parade*. He befriended Olga Kohkhlova, a ballerina in the troupe, whom he married in 1918 and whose portraits he painted in great numbers. These, as well as those of his first son Paulo, are full of realism.

1935 Picasso split with his wife Olga as he pursued his relationship with Marie-Thérèse Walter, whom he had met in 1927 and was now expecting a daughter, Maya. He became close to André Breton and the surrealists and began to write poems in French and Spanish. He continued this activity until the end of the 1950s. He painted the mythical figure of the Minotaur along with bullfights and still lifes.

1937 Following the bombing of the small Basque town of Guernica, he painted the eponymous picture. Dora Maar, a newcomer to his life, and of whom the artist made many portraits, documented the conception of the work. Left in storage since 1939 at the Museum of Modern Art in New York, *Guernica* would not return to Spain until 1981. The sordid years of the war influenced the artist's production: colors darkened, cats devoured birds, bull skulls combined with candles and books called for a meditation on death. After the war, his "dove of peace" would become a symbol of peace.

1948 Picasso moved to Vallauris in the South of France with his new partner, Françoise Gilot, an artist herself and mother of two of his children, Claude and Paloma. Hosted by the Ramié couple in their Madoura studio, Picasso devoted himself to ceramics. He also moved into a new studio where he made numerous sculptures. Towards the middle of the 1950s, Picasso started creating works inspired by the masterpieces of the great masters (Velázquez, Manet, Delacroix, etc.).

1958 He moved to the Château de Vauvenargues in the South of France, then in 1961, to Notre-Dame-de-Vie, in Mougins with Jacqueline Roque, who became his wife.

1963 Inauguration of the Museu Picasso in Barcelona. The "last period" of Picasso's work multiplies the representations of musketeers, matadors, families and maternities.

1973 Death of Picasso in Mougins.

ACKNOWLEDGMENTS

Éditions Skira would like to thank Encore Productions and especially Pascal Bernardin, as well as the directors of "Imagine Picasso" Annabelle Mauger and Julien Baron, for their involvement. This project would not have been possible without them, and may they receive our deepest gratitude.

Our thanks also go to Androula Michael for her texts and her precious collaboration throughout the realization of this work.

We would also like to thank the Picasso Administration and especially Christine Pinault for her support.

We are very grateful to all those who helped us during this work and especially to the photographers, Lisa Ricciotti and Laurence Labat.

Annabelle and Julien would also like to thank Claire Couriol and the entire team at La Sucrière for having supported this project from the start, as well as the Canadian teams for their constant commitment.

Finally, Annabelle would like to thank Rudy Ricciotti for having accompanied her with so much determination for so many years and for having been able to meet the challenge of dialoguing with Picasso.

COPYRIGHTS

Unless otherwise stated, all works are:
© Succession Picasso

Photographic credits:
Unless otherwise stated, all photographs are:
© Laurence Labat

Cover and pp. 44–45, 52–53: © Lisa Ricciotti

pp. 36–37: © lililillilil

p. 60 (from left to right):
© RMN-Grand Palais (Musée National Picasso-Paris) / Mathieu Rabeau
© Javier Larrea
© Archives Alinari, Florence, Dist. RMN-Grand Palais / Fratelli Alinari
© The Philadelphia Museum of Art, Dist. RMN-Grand Palais / image Philadelphia Museum of Art
© RMN-Grand Palais (Musée National Picasso-Paris) / Mathieu Rabeau
© RMN-Grand Palais (Musée National Picasso-Paris) / Mathieu Rabeau
© RMN-Grand Palais (Musée National Picasso-Paris) / Adrien Didierjean
© BPK, Berlin, Dist. RMN-Grand Palais / Alfredo Dagli Orti
© RMN-Grand Palais (Musée National Picasso-Paris) / Mathieu Rabeau

p. 61 (from left to right):
© The Museum of Modern Art, New York / Scala, Florence, 2019
© Archives Alinari, Florence, Dist. RMN Grand Palais / Fratelli Alinari
© Centre Pompidou, MNAM-CCI, Dist. RMN-Grand Palais / Christian Bahier / Philippe Migeat
© RMN-Grand Palais (Musée National Picasso-Paris) / Mathieu Rabeau
© The Museum of Modern Art, New York / Scala, Florence, 2019
© RMN-Grand Palais (Musée National Picasso-Paris) / Mathieu Rabeau
© RMN-Grand Palais (Musée National Picasso-Vallauris) / Patrick Gérin
© akg-images / Album / Kocinsky

p. 62 and back cover: © Michel Mako / Gamma-Rapho via Getty Images

SKIRA PARIS

14 rue Serpente, 75006 Paris
www.skira.net

Senior editor
Nathalie Prat-Couadau

Editorial coordination
María Laura Ribadeneira

Project manager
Meryl Mason

Publishing assistant
Anna Koch

Graphic design
Sophie Dupriez

Proofreading
Myriam Birch

Colour separation
Litho Art New, Turin

Printed by Graphius–Geers Offset in Ghent, Belgium, December 2021